STRESS AND TH[...]

An analysis of how tension ma[...]
a deeper understanding of as[...]logical types and
through a unique development of traditional sun sign
interpretations.

STRESS
—AND THE—
SUN SIGNS

An astrological approach to the
self-treatment of tension

by

RUPERT J. SEWELL

THE AQUARIAN PRESS
Wellingborough, Northamptonshire

First published 1981

British Library Cataloguing in Publication Data

Sewell, Rupert
  Stress and the sun signs.
  1. Medical astrology   2. Stress (Psychology)
  I. Title
  133.58'816'89

  ISBN 0-85030-241-2

Typeset by Harper Phototypesetters, Northampton
Printed in Great Britain by
Lowe and Brydone Printers Ltd., Thetford, Norfolk,
and bound by Weatherby Woolnough, Wellingborough,
Northamptonshire.

CONTENTS

The personal responsibility of the astrologer to his clients, his friends or hearers reveals itself conclusively as one deals with the source of practically all negative psychological factors: fear.

Dane Rudhyar, *The Practice of Astrology.*

INTRODUCTION

A good deal of misinformation has been presented to the public about astrology, and the sun signs in particular, that it has taken me some considerable time, and not a little courage, to decide to commit my thoughts and findings to paper. Several reasons eventually spurred me into making the attempt to do so. Firstly, I have always felt the desire to relieve human suffering, from my early days in wartime hospitals, through my years of consultative work, and up to the present time, when the ever increasing pressures within society as a whole makes it all too evident that stress is, perhaps, the chief cause for the undermining of health, as well as producing anxiety and tension.

Also, at long last, there have been advances in astrology at the scientific level, to the extent that eminent men, like Professor H. J. Eysenck, have contributed significantly to research in the subject, enabling serious astrologers to feel that the time has at last come when a proper understanding and acceptance of astrology is possible. It was the publication of a paper on astrological and psychological correlations by Mayo and Eysenck that encouraged me to pursue investigations of my own, resulting in a list of personality types and tendencies that had more in-depth detail than has hitherto been possible when information has been derived solely from the sun signs. This means that we now have a reasonably reliable personality reference—always allowing for the fact that there must still be some degree of generalization in having to refer to only one factor—with which to make a rapid assessment of individual tendencies and motivations.

It is not my intention to confuse the general reader with the technical jargon of astrology or psychology, but there is such a wide interest in both these subjects that I shall endeavour to explain the fundamentals regarding current understanding in both disciplines. It is my hope that this book will go some way towards alleviating the condition we know as stress or tension, and that the list of personality types—placed at a logical position within the book—will enable you to gain a deeper understanding of yourself far more easily and rapidly than relying on standard methods of psychological assessment.

The use of astrology as an aid and a palliative, even in a modest way, is both reasonable and natural. Mankind forever seeks to find himself *outside* himself. For example, popular magazines and journals often carry features comprising a set of questions, designed to reveal something about yourself in the way you answer. For instance, whether you are successful in love, in your career, mixing with others, and so on. Colour, too, provides an interesting medium for self-analysis. Just the other day my wife showed me the heading of an article she was reading. It stated: 'Psycho-Fashion Special—What your colour choice reveals about you'. One way or another, then, the mass media panders to an inherent and universal need within human beings—to be able to discover themselves.

Sun sign astrology falls into the same category. Almost every newspaper and periodical throughout the world carries some form of 'Your Stars', or 'The Zodiac and You'. Maybe you agree that the sun signs reveal something of a person's nature, or maybe you do not; but what is very clear is that there is an inborn, instinctive urge in each one of us, to seek for greater understanding of ourselves and to reach for the hidden springs of our totality.

How To Use This Book

In Self-Help

If you have already had a glance at the personality classifications (p. 27), please do remember that it is a list of probabilities, not of descriptions of fixed behaviour patterns. It is placed in a logical position within the book, so that it can be utilized with the greatest understanding of its function as an aid. Try to read on with patience. As an understanding of the condition of stress as a whole increases, so will tensions decrease.

This book is not intended to deal with severe cases of anxiety, though the insights provided can enable anyone to improve their perspective of themselves and their condition, so that they may be in a better position to decide whether or not to seek for further guidance. Be assured that any gain of understanding into one's actual situation or condition is a real advantage. No matter how weak, insecure or uncertain we may feel, each one of us has inner resources far in excess of any immediate demands. The sun shines from within as well as without, although at times clouds of self-doubt obscure it from the inner vision.

For Those in Social Services

Today, many people working in the community services (teachers, probation officers, social workers, therapists, etc.) take a serious view of astrology. Social and community workers deal with human needs and problems daily, and any means of gaining deeper understanding of personality patterns and motivations can be an advantage—as well as a real time-saver. Clearly, it is those who, in some way, are having to employ a knowledge of psychology in their dealings with others who will find the list of personality tendencies of most help. For this reason I have included a chapter that goes a little further into the psychological implications involved, because most of the observations made in the interpretations are based upon underlying principles, the understanding of which can provide rather more information than may at first be thought possible.

Obviously, it is not to be expected that such a list will be other than an aid only, ancillary to whatever routine methods of assessment are already in use. However, a brief indication as to the validity of the interpretations can be conveyed in the summary of a senior consultant psychiatrist who, after checking it as thoroughly as possible, deemed its effectiveness as an accurate measure of probable personality tendencies as varying from very good to extremely good.

Students of Astrology

The method developed for interpreting the sun's ecliptical movement, while apparently simple in its presentation, evolved only gradually. Because I believe it to be unique, possibly a minor breakthrough in the interpretation of archetypal structures, I am including a description of the process involved which you may like to try for yourself. If my observations encourage further research and experimentation, so much the better; for it is only through the patient pursuit of every channel of the science that the sum total of knowledge can be increased. Astrology, as a science, has made great strides in the last few years, and there is more than sufficient evidence to support its concepts, certainly at the more complex levels of individual birth chart analysis.

To the General Reader

Quite apart from any fresh thought or guidance that this book may impart to you, the very fact that you are prepared to read something of an astrological nature suggests an ability to accept the broad concepts of the subject, and this, to me at least, is most encouraging. It means that you are able to accept yourself; for what is astrology if it is not a reflection of Mankind's total experience?

Being able to accept ourselves means being able to step back with humility, acknowledge our weaknesses, and perceive how small we are, as individuals, in relationship to the vastness of time and space. It is not easy for everyone to do this, and indeed many become frightened at the mere thought of it. These are the ones who most often give themselves away by acting in a cynical or even antagonistic manner whenever astrology—and quite often, psychology too—is mentioned. No one goes on the defensive or the attack unless they are, unconsciously, very frightened or insecure within themselves. But not for nothing did Christ teach us to 'Love thy neighbour as thyself'. Love starts in the innermost heart and inevitably radiates outwards, while fear isolates, puts up Iron Curtains, starts wars!

Stress is a symptom of the general malaise within our modern society; but it is also a stimulus to action, and I would like to think that through a conscious effort of self-discovery by the individual, the true values and creative forces of society could be realized in greater measure, for the general good.

1. WHAT IS STRESS?

Very few of us escape stress, indeed a modicum of it in our lives is a necessary stimulus to overcoming the challenges of life. Some of us can withstand more than others, and most of us think little about it until such time as it makes itself felt. Even then we are disinclined to stop and contemplate the very thing that is producing the discomfort. After all, it is only natural to try and avoid anything that is disturbing or that appears to threaten us.

If it is true that we tend to run away from something we are afraid of, it is equally true that we are likely to be more afraid of what is unknown. Something that we can understand or find an explanation for ceases to be quite so fearsome. This reasoning can apply not only to the stress condition, but to our own natures as well; for it is quite common to feel anxious and uncertain about those parts of ourselves that we cannot immediately understand or accept. The first step, then, is to de-mystify the condition we call stress.

We must first be clear about the terms we use. Stress, tension, worry or anxiety all arise from the same root—fear. That is the nettle we have to grasp, and, just like the nettle, if grasped firmly it is much less likely to sting. How can we do this?

More often than not we tend to blame our situation and the circumstances we find ourselves in for all those disturbing feelings of inner tension. So we need to pause and consider whether the situation is really as dangerous or as threatening as we *feel* it is. This is such a fundamental consideration that it is often overlooked; yet here, at once, you have a clue to right understanding about the stress condition. Obviously, we all feel through our body mechanisms, and feelings colour our thoughts. If we *feel* frightened we eventually come to think that we are in some way endangered. The actual feelings of tension and anxiety arise from *physical responses,* not from the situation.

Biological Responses

But why should our bodies respond in tense, uncomfortable and disquieting ways? Because, in the dawn of time, when the conditions of living could be resolved into simple terms of whether one was the hunter or the hunted, survival meant physical adaptation, or extinction. So it was that the human body evolved as a complex organism, conditioned to certain basic reflexes. These are widely known and are often described as the tendencies for 'Fright, fight, or flight'.

Under the stimulus of a threat to its security the body gears itself up for action and prepares for defence. Biochemically, our batteries are put on full charge, and we have a surplus of energy, ready to wield that club, or run helter-skelter through the jungle scrub.

Most of us have heard someone exclaim, 'It got the old adrenalin going!', or something similar to that, meaning that a particularly exciting or dangerous experience has keyed the individual up for action. It need not be a particularly unpleasant situation for the body's normal responses to be triggered. There are many, for example, who enjoy the thrill of a potentially dangerous sport. But either way, whether from fear or excitement, the physical response is the same. Adrenalin enters the bloodstream, increasing the pulse-rate, and the blood vessels near the surface of the skin contract. This is nature's way of conserving blood in the event of injury and accounts for why we feel cold and clammy when we are anxious or worried by something.

When we feel anxious, our muscles also begin to tighten up. This is another normal response and prepares the body for violent physical exertion. This, of course, is unlikely in our modern environment, unless we are going to take part in some active exercise. More often than not, the amount of anxiety is slight and so we hardly notice the underlying tension in the muscles. But it is there, especially in the stomach muscles, giving rise to a sinking feeling, or 'butterflies in the tummy'.

In my experience, one thing that worries people most is the pounding of their hearts when under stress. For those who do suffer in this way, it is reassuring to remember that the heart is the strongest muscle in the body. Even if you forced yourself to the limits of physical endurance, you would simply drop from fatigue long before any damage could be done to the heart. All physiological responses are self-limiting. The body takes care of itself automatically. Even the experience of 'missing a beat' is such a common occurence as to be considered normal. You can always check with your doctor if you still have any doubts about this. (Dr Claire Weekes covers this aspect of anxiety very adequately. See bibliography.)

The symptoms of stress can create further anxieties of their own. A vicious circle can be started up because of this, and that is why it really does pay to pause, relax, and consciously seek to accept what are, in fact, normal physical responses. This is something we shall go into further in Chapter Four.

When it comes to the type of behaviour human beings are likely to exhibit under stress, we have seen that fright stimulates us to either fight, or to take flight. These tendencies are so well known that over the years various descriptions have been applied to them by researchers. For example: 'aggressive and compliant', 'tough and soft', 'extravertive and introvertive'. Of course, all such classifications are very broad. The individual personality is far too complex to be seen as all one thing or another; but at least such simplified descriptions of the fundamentals of personality and behaviour do provide a useful working basis for better understanding.

In the researches carried out by Mayo and Eysenck (enlarged upon later), a successful attempt was made to demonstrate the correlation between sun signs and the two well-known classifications of extravertism and introvertism. It was this work which provided a basis for the list of thirty-six personality types and tendencies given in Chapter Three.

During the process of growth, the trunk of a tree in a forest will often twist this way and that in order to reach the light. Fully-grown, the tree may give the appearance of carrying the weight of its branches awkwardly, as though under stress, because of the angular distortion. Our personalities, especially when young and tender, bend, adapt and modify in order to survive and grow in society. When a great deal of adaptation has taken place, albeit instinctively and unconsciously, some of the burdens or pressures of life may not be carried quite so easily, and a sense of tension or stress results. It is easy to see which branches of the tree need support. It is not always easy to determine where, and why, in the personality the stresses occur. That is why any reasonable system of personality assessment is valuable as a guide to deeper insight into the self.

2. SELF-ANALYSIS AND PERSONALITY TENDENCIES

The various methods of personality assessment in current use often require a good deal of time to apply and someone trained in their interpretation to extract the necessary information. The list of thirty-six types and tendencies given here will enable you to make an assessment rapidly and easily. It is most effective if you can be honest with yourself. At one of my classes, after everyone had been through the list for themselves, I asked one student if it agreed with what he knew of himself. With a grin, he replied, 'All the positive traits, yes. All the negative ones, no!'.

If you are undertaking any form of self-help for the relief of tension and stres you have to be prepared to take an honest look at the apparent weaknesses. There is no need to feel any trepidation about this. It is the truth that releases us from our misconceptions about ourselves.

Using The List

Some readers may be unfamiliar with the sun signs, and for this reason a complete list has been included. This follows the usual procedure of giving interpretations to the twelve monthly birth periods, i.e., the signs of the Zodiac, as used in popular astrology.

People who happen to be born just at a time of the month when the sun is moving from one sign into another are often puzzled as to why their sun signs change from magazine to magazine. The reason for this is simply because of the effect of leap years and the astrologer-writer's dilemma in the choice of monthly dates. If your birth date does happen to be near a sign change, read the interpretations that fall either side. You should be able to see at once which applies.

Remember, the list is a guide to *probable* tendencies, not all of which can be expected to apply to any one person. From lengthy checking it has been shown to have a reasonably high validity rate, but it would be incorrect to think that it could be applied correctly invariably. Here are a few examples of how the list can be used to aid self-understanding:

Marilyn Monroe

Marilyn Monroe, film idol, whose marriage and tragic end are well known, was born on 1 June. In popular astrological parlance she would be termed a 'Gemini', and therefore considered to be versatile, communicative, quick-witted, lively, superficial, and so on. However, if we turn to the list and find the section in which her birth date falls, not only is there an indication of the general traits, albeit briefly stated (the general characteristics are expanded upon in the preliminary list called 'Signs of the Zodiac'), but also what is, in fact, the underlying principle that tends to modify the general characteristics. It will be seen that Geminians born in this particular period of the month may tend to orientate via their relationships. Therefore, the feeling or affectional nature is an important consideration, but something which might be entirely overlooked if one were to rely upon the more generalized interpretations of the Zodiac. Geminis, we are also told, love finding out, need mental stimulus, do not like being tied down. Introduce the idea of a need for love and affection into this generalized conception of a 'thinking type' and we have a whole new dimension. Thinking and feeling are opposite functions within the personality. Usually, thinkers prefer to rely upon their intellect and reasoning rather than on their feelings. In fact, strong feelings may disturb or frighten them.

Thus, as in this instance, where we have a combination of thinking and feeling it is as if there is a continual flux within the person, producing mood swings, restlessness and uncertainty whenever relationship problems come to the fore.

Here is another example.

Margaret Thatcher

Mrs Margaret Thatcher, British Prime Minister, was born on 13 October and is therefore, a sun Libran. If we go by the generally accepted view of this sign we might think of 'lazy Libra', easy-going, liking pleasant surroundings and company, a desire for maintaining harmony with others, and hating to burden themselves with difficult or irksome tasks. Certainly, a tendency towards self-esteem is inherent in the sign as a whole, but you will find little written about Libra that conveys the idea of a self-motivating drive to succeed, or meet challenges; and yet this is an underlying feature of those who happen to be born in this particular part of the month. The sign Libra has reference to harmonious relationships or social awareness, though the underlying factor referred to in the list interpretation is one of self-will and independence of expression. Hence, should any tension or stress within the personality become apparent, it would have to do with the struggle between what the individual wants and what the individual feels is acceptable to others—that all too common pull between pleasing oneself and having to consider others at the same time. Mrs Thatcher, and indeed anyone born in this period of the month, will be motivated by a strong sense of independence that has to be assimilated into the total personality in an harmonious (Libran) manner.

In these two examples we have a vivid illustration of how people can utilize what may appear to be conflicting tendencies within the nature to enable them to live their lives to the full. In the first one, fruition of the potential came about tragically early, yet a great deal had been achieved, and the name of Marilyn Monroe will long remain a legend. In the second case, Mrs Thatcher attained high office through constructive channelling of the inherent drives set up by conflicting elements of her nature.

An Average Case

Born 16 April, our average case is in his forties, works in an office, and has already had a heart attack. If we turn to the list, it is possible to get some idea of why he has suffered in this way. Clearly, the Arien drive is there, though we see that the self-assertion of Aries has given way to a feeling of wanting to enthuse and impress, rather than assert the self. Therefore, in this sector of the sign it is more a desire for acceptance than a full-blooded 'Me first' attitude.

If you were to meet this man, however, you would see a quiet, self-effacing individual, who gives no indication of enterprise or enthusiasm, although he was lively and enjoyed sport when young. His life has been difficult, and perhaps the pressures of earning a living and maintaining a family have been too restrictive to the naturally lively temperament, which, over the years, has become repressed. And a sedentary life for one who basically requires plenty of outlets for the abundant energy will also have had its effect. Possibly, too, frustrated enthusiasm has lead to a building-up of resentment in not having been able to play out his life in the way he would have liked to have done. If so, this would have increased the possibility of inner tensions, eventually producing high blood pressure, and culminating, in this particular instance, in a heart attack.

Consideration of this case leads to the question of whether emotional (or physical) crises can be avoided if an individual had achieved greater insight into his true personality potential earlier in life. Clearly, dis-ease arises out of a lack of ease, or harmony. We must perceive, understand and nurture all that is true to ourselves, in order that we may fulfil our potentialities. Our own unique service and contribution to society is worthy in itself, no matter how great or small it may be.

Positive and Negative Tendencies

For those who are interested, the references to the underlying principles are enlarged upon in Chapter Five. A few words need to be said here, however, about the positive and negative tendencies. Any symbolism that has evolved from Man's desire to understand himself and his function within the universe must inevitably reflect the laws of nature. One of the most fundamental of these is that everything has an opposite: night and day, black and white, hot and cold, male and female, conscious and unconscious, and so on. There is a constant flux and struggle to maintain the balance of nature, and this is no less true for the individual personality than it is for the whole of life.

'Positive' and 'negative', in the context used here, are simply terms of convenience; for nothing is all black or all white, but usually varying shades of grey. The positive qualities may be thought of as those which are most widely acknowledged as being acceptable to ourselves and others. Negative tendencies are those same qualities taken to extremes. For example, generosity can become extravagance, liveliness turn to impatience and irritability, or stability to unmoving obstinacy.

It is worth considering, too, that the polar opposite of action is non-action. Extreme physical activity has the obvious consequence —a desire for rest. Too much emphasis upon a particular feeling or function can result in an instinctive move to counter it in order to restore balance and harmony. The explanation for this can be found at the physiological as well as the psychological level. There is a homoeopathic observation (the Arndt-Schultz Law) that states: 'Small stimuli encourage life activity. Medium stimuli impede life activity. Strong stimuli stop or destroy life activity'. If we read 'stress' for 'stimuli' the idea is quite relevant here. Our negative tendencies, which are prone to, or the result of, over-stimulus, can be modified, eased, balanced, and compensated for by greater awareness of positive tendencies that we might well have lost sight of. By the same token, a clearer understanding of our tendencies, as a whole, plays an essential part in gaining a truer perspective of ourselves.

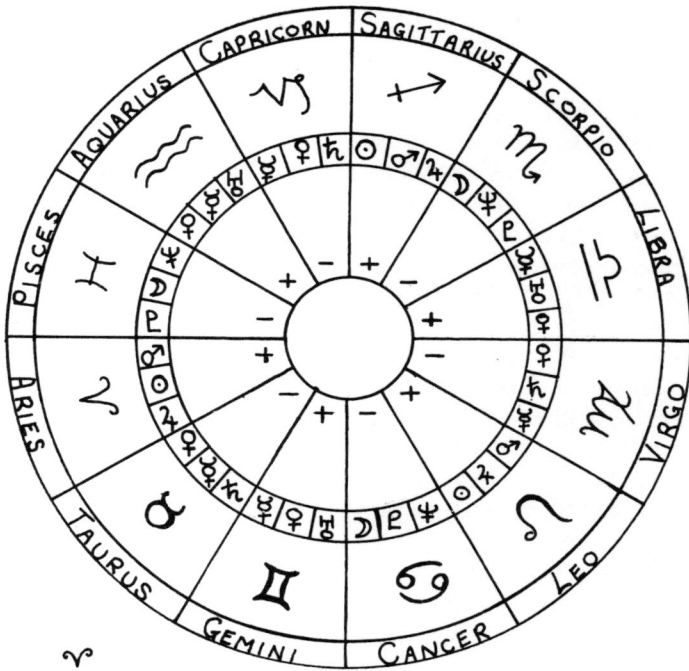

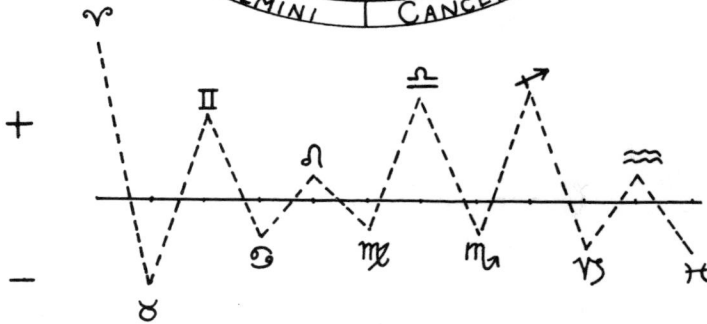

The sequence of signs is read anti-clockwise, from Aries to Pisces. Each sign has its sub-division of planetary principles, and its complimentary or opposite. Traditionally, each sign has the designation of positivity or negativity. The graph underneath the Wheel illustrates the alternation of certain personality characteristics, as dependent upon the month of birth, and you can find the reference to this on page 24.

THE SIGNS OF THE ZODIAC

Aries: 21 March-20 April
+ Active, assertive and initiating. Often passionate, and likes to feel causative. Tends to operate through force of will.
— Can become hasty, impatient, quarrelsome, over-aggressive.

The sign has traditional reference to: butchers, soldiers, engineers, pioneers. Fire, spirit, energy.

Tissue-salt: Kali Phos. (Potassium phosphate).

Taurus: 21 April-21 May
+ Stable, practical and enduring. Finds contentment in physical comfort and pleasures. Often preservering in earning and acquiring in order to maintain sense of security.
— Can become over-passive, obstinate, and/or subjectively concerned with material values.

The sign has traditional reference to: farming, money (hard cash), music—singing in particular. Earth, materiality, inertia.

Tissue-salt: Nat. Sulph. (Sodium Sulphate).

Gemini: 22 May-21 June
+ Investigatory, and keen to find out. Adaptable, eager and versatile.
— Can become too restless, superficial, changeable.

The sign has traditional reference to: air, intellect, communication, speaking, writing, transport.

Tissue-salt: Kali Mur. (Potassium Chloride).

Cancer: 22 June-23 July
+ Usually sensitive, and of a caring, nurturing disposition. Often has a strong sense of family, and can be sympathetic and understanding of the needs of others.
— Over-sensitive response to the influence of others and the ups and downs of daily life can produce vacillation, moodiness.

The sign has traditional reference to: mother, home, water, stomach, catering, shipping.

Tissue-salt: Calc. Fluor. (Calcium Fluoride).

Leo: 24 July-23 August
+ Assured, confident, creative and/or organizing disposition. Aspiring, projective, and pleasure-loving. Likes entertainment and gambling.
— Can become too ego-centred, over-confident, and may resent interference.

The sign has traditional reference to: fire, finance (speculation), amusements, drama (the stage).

Tissue-salt: Mag. Phos. (Magnesium Phosphate).

Virgo: 24 August-23 September
Methodical, practical, appreciates orderliness. Often attracted to learning, and to aquiring technical ability. May be of an analytical disposition.
— May become over-critical of self, and others, and anxious about attention to detail—fussy.

The sign has traditional reference to: earth, practical knowledge, purity, health, hygiene, secretaries, librarians.

Tissue-salt: Kali Sulph. (Potassium Sulphate).

Libra: 24 September—23 October
+ Usually has charm and sociability. Seeks agreeable surroundings and associations in which to achieve acknowledgement of personal value. Adaptable.
— Sometimes indecisive, and may become too vacillating, or too easily discouraged by lack of accord.

The sign has traditional reference to: air, associations, partnerships, good taste, agents, jewellers, fashion.

Tissue-salt: Nat. Phos. (Sodium Phosphate).

Scorpio: 24 October-22 November
+ Striving and persistent in seeking for control at physical and emotional levels. Usually has a marked degree of sense-perception; sensual; tenacious.
— Intensity of feelings could result in over-estimation of ability, or a misguided attitude.

The sign has traditional reference to: water, deep penetration, hidden depths, police, psychiatrists and psychologists, strong emotional forces.

Tissue-salt: Calc. Sulph. (Calcium Sulphate).

Sagittarius: 23 November-22 December

+ Active, enthusiastic, and idealistic. Often gregarious and freedom-loving.

— Can become over-imaginative, prone to extravagances, lacking in foresight, or absent-minded.

The sign has traditional reference to: fire, mobility, prophecy, philosophy, religion, law, publishers.

Tissue-salt: Silica (Silica Oxide).

Capricorn: 23 December-20 January

+ Conservative and industrious. Usually has patience in attaining objectives. Ambitious. Needs a sense of security and is prepared to work hard to achieve it.

— May place too much emphasis upon career interests at the expense of other things. Can become one-sided, over-serious.

The sign has traditional reference to: earth, lead, skeleton and skin, governmental structures, managers, time, limitations.

Tissue-salt: Calc. Phos. (Calcium Phosphate).

Aquarius: 21 January-19 February

+ Friendly though individualistic and something of a reformer. Appreciates a sense of independence, but usually holds strong humanitarian views.

— If too confined by convention, may become restless, rebellious, and self-willed.

The sign has traditional reference to: air, dissemination of knowledge, rhythmic wave-patterns, e.g., radio, light-waves; music, clubs and associations, circulation.

Tissue-salt: Nat. Mur. (Sodium Chloride).

Pisces: 20 February-20 March

+ Receptive and intuitive. May incline to the spiritual, artistic, and inner spheres of consciousness. Often attracted to quiet, secluded places.

— Can become too impressionable, or tend to withdraw from reality—something of a dreamer.

The sign has traditional reference to: water, vapour, gases, alcohol, acting, art, hospitals and institutions, feet.

Tissue-salt: Ferr. Phos. (Iron Phosphate).

The preceding list is no more than a résumé of the essential qualities of the sun signs for those who have no previous knowledge of them. For anyone wishing to read more on the subject there are scores of books dealing exclusively with the astrological correlations. Some titles are given in the bibliography.

PERSONALITY TENDENCIES

+ = the generally observable tendencies.

— = likely types of tendencies more noticeable under stress.

Birth Date   *Tendencies*

1-10 January: + Feels a need for harmony, security and constancy in relationships. Pursues selected objectives with zeal.

— Unsatisfactory relationships, or frustrating conditions may produce suppressed agitation, irritability. May become prone to obsessive tendencies, could become prone to sexual neuroses.

11-20 January: + Thinking is serious or deliberative. Desires to solve problems, especially those that threaten security. Usually industrious and aspiring.

— Conditions causing uncertainty or frustration to the ambitions give rise to anxiety. Can develop a feeling of loneliness or depression. There may be a tendency to take too narrow a view, become obstinate. May be liable to self-deception, or put on an air of reserve or unconcern, in an effort to cover feelings of anxiety or inadequacy.

21-30 January: + Strongly individualistic, and strives to overcome all obstacles in the gaining of recognition.

— Can be sensitive to stress situations. May fear emotional involvements. Frustration produces impatience, tension, contrariness, leading to self-willed or rebellious behaviour. May become prone to muscular tension/spasm, and or circulatory troubles.

A hyper-sensitive, perhaps aggressive response is sometimes observable in those born close to the 21st.

31 January-   + Usually keenly observant with an alert mind.
9 February: Is enthusiastic and often has a lively imagination. Seeks for mental stimuli and wider fields of interest which could increase the chances for recognition and success.

— Unfulfilled aspirations and disappointments could produce a loss of concentration, vacillation, and perhaps a resentful or negligent attitude.

10-19 February: + Usually, keen, eager and alert. Can be self-willed in affectional matters, because of an inner need to preserve a sense of self-containment and independence.

— Unsatisfactory relationships may lead to impatience, contrariness, vacillation. Self-will, if engendering excessive tension, may eventually undermine sense of perseverance, and could affect the circulation and/or fluid balance.

There is some likelihood of hypersensitive response to be found in those born between the 12th and 17th.

20-29 February: + Usually very receptive to environmental influences and atmosphere. Often imaginative, and can be attracted to areas of fantasy and abstract concepts.

— If over-imaginative, there is an increased possibility for self-deception, or lack of clarity in viewing the motives of others. Difficulties and disappointments could lead to an inclination to withdraw from reality. And, with those born near to the 24th, there may be some tendency to repression and/or psychosomatic (physical, e.g., asthma) response.

1-10 March: + There is usually a desire to be well-liked. Wants an interesting, fascinating life. Is often imaginative, but also likely to be concerned about practicalities and security.

— Difficulties in relationships or conditions may give rise to an over-cautious, circumspect behaviour pattern. Is inclined to become over-conscientious, resulting in anxiety from which depression could develop. Would require security and freedom from worry.

11-20 March: + Responsive and susceptible to stimuli. Is often attracted to anything that can provide excitement and intensification of feelings—which includes the erotic.

— Difficulties in relationships can arise from an intensity of feelings (sexual). May become obsessive. Undue suppression of the feelings could lead to agitation, irritability, neuroses, and some tendency to withdraw.

21-31 March: + Usually, an active and ardent individual, and often of an enterprising nature. Seeks for satisfaction in close relationships.

— Disharmony in relationships brings about impatience, irritability, anger, and when prolonged, sexual problems may develop. Anxiety could be produced if having to suppress the excitable, ardent nature.
Some hypersensitivity of response, perhaps expressed as aggresiveness, may be discernible in those born close to the 26th.

1-10 April: + Active and often restless, ardent, and individualistic. May seek to assert self, and strive to overcome all obstacles in order to achieve recognition or success.

— Unsatisfactory relationships can produce impatience, irritability, anger. Supression of the strong libido (emotional—sexual drive) could give rise to tension, impulsive behaviour, neuroses.
There may be some increased likelihood of hypersensitive (perhaps aggressive) response, and/or hypertension (high blood pressure) to be found in those born near to the 5th.

11-20 April: + Vigorous, enterprising and enthusiastic. May seek to impress personality on others. Often desires excitement in the life—mental and physical stimuli.

— Frustration or disappointments may give rise to impetuous, perhaps negligent, type of behaviour. Anxiety is produced when the natural drive and enthusiasm are suppressed.

21-30 April: + Usually has deep-seated feelings. Tends to seek for harmonious and satisfying relationships. Needs the reassurance of physical and material security.

— Emotional upsets may give rise to inhibition or suppression of the sexual-urge, irritability. Obsessive tendencies may develop.

1-11 May: + Deliberative, though usually intuitive. Seeks for a harmonious and stable environment.

— Frustrations or disappointments may give rise to day-dreaming, seeking for physical comforts. Can become one-sided, prone to self-deception, suffer from inertia.
Some nervous sensitivity may be apparent in those born close to the 1st.
Hypersensitivity, perhaps tending towards obsessiveness, may be apparent in those born near to the 7th.

12-21 May: + Quietly persevering. Seeks for material security and physical ease. Desires satisfying, enduring relationships.

— May present a show of stolid self-reliance in order to cover emotional upsets or disappointments. There may be a fear of loneliness or inadequacy which prompts this. Under difficult circumstances, depression may develop.

22-31 May: + Alert, keenly observant, and usually of an enthusiastic nature. Seeks for mental stimuli, and an appreciation of abilities.

— Over-enthusiasm may lead to a lack of foresight. Frustrations can bring about tension, vacillation, irritability, negligence. A restless impatience is also possible.

Those born near to the 28th may tend towards nervousness.

1-11 June: + Eager and alert, with a lively awareness. May seek for the approbation of others, and might use charm to achieve this.

— Conflicts and tensions could arise through superficiality of love attachments. Difficulties and disappointments can lead to mood changes, and perhaps inhibition of the love-expression. May lack confidence or suffer through feelings of insecurity. Some hypersensitivity and/or impulsiveness may be more apparent in those born close to the 8th and 9th, and there could also be an increased tendency towards psychosomatic (physical reaction: e.g., asthma) response.

12-21 June: + Observant, and ever alert to new interests that can offer scope and recognition of intellectual (very often) abilities. Aspiring, rather than overtly ambitious, though can vacillate through diversity of interests/ objectives.

— Vulnerable to stress, and prone to nervous tension. May scatter energies, act too hastily under pressure, in an effort to circumvent difficulties. Frustration in the pursuit of interest may lead to irritability, impatience.

Those born near to the 17th appear to have an increased likelihood of an over-active nervous system. Extra tensions may there-fore produce anxiety and/or desire to withdraw from mental stimuli.

22 June-2 July   + Usually of a caring and conscientious disposition. There is a marked emotional content. May seek for a secure environment

in which there is love, and freedom from loneliness and anxiety. Needs to give as well as receive tender loving care. Sometimes circumspect, and can impose self-restraint.

— Disappointment in relationships may give rise to an assumed indifference, though there is a tendency to become depressed when faced with isolation and/or insecurity. Anxiety could also arise through over-conscientiousness.

3-12 July: + Emotionally restless, and needs to feel causative. May search for new fields of endeavour. Can pursue an interest, or a love-attachment, with intensity. Desires to make a favourable impression.

— May become distressed and anxious by difficulties in relationships and disappointments, which could lead to irritability, unrealistic self-justification, sexual neuroses. May develop an obsessive tendency.

13-23 July: + Intuitive, sensitive and imaginative. Can be highly receptive, and sympathetic to the feelings of others.

— Over-receptiveness and imaginativeness could make for a lack of clarity in regarding the motives of others, self-deception, and/or an inclination to withdraw from reality.

24 July-2 August: + Active, projective. Seeks for self-expression, and strives to overcome all obstacles in order to achieve recognition and success.

— Could develop an obsessive tendency in striving to achieve recognition. Vacillation, impatience, anxiety and tension are all possible when efforts are thwarted. There may be a tendency, when under pressure, to work until collapse. Could develop circulatory/cardiac troubles. Those born near to the 23rd sometimes appear to be more prone to hypertension and egocentric behaviour patterns.

3-13 August:
+ Responsive to anything that is stimulating and enjoyable. Usually confident and socially aspiring/ambitious. Seeks recognition and popularity.

— May overestimate self. Stress arises from difficulties in achieving recognition or success. Could become absent-minded or off-hand. In failure, might resent the apparent success of others.

14-23 August:
+ Active, enterprising, and usually able to take the initiative. Seeks for recognition of talents, security, and satisfaction in relationships.

— May fear rejection and loneliness, though may dislike being restricted by others. Unsatisfactory relationships could give rise to irritability, angry frustration, perhaps sexual problems. Disappointments may bring about lack of confidence, depression.
   Those born close to the 16th may sometimes appear to over-react, e.g., possibly over-excitable, impulsive.

24 August-
2 September:
+ Practical thinking in the search for secure conditions is usually evident. Pursues objectives with quiet hopefulness and sensibility. Seeks for harmonious cooperation with others.

— Might try to conceal worry with a show of modest efficiency. Desires sympathetic understanding. May try to avoid emotional conflicts.

There would seem to be more likelihood of repressive and/or psychosomatic tendencies in those born near the 28th.

3-13 September: + Serious, thorough and discreet. Tends to seek for security and freedom from worry.

— Can become over-conscientious, and therefore prone to anxiety. Some tendency to depression. Difficulties in relationships may give rise to inhibitions, feelings of inadequacy, possibly sexual problems. Could develop an over-critical attitude. Liable to put on a show of self-reliance in order to cover feelings of anxiety. Some tendency to worry about health/diet.

14-23 September: + The affectional nature may sometimes be over-ruled by practical/moral considerations. An underlying intensity of feeling may provide the spur to seek for new fields of endeavour which can offer greater opportunities for personal significance.

— Ther may be a vacillation in love matters, and difficulties in close relationships can give rise to nervousness, agitation, irritability, sexual neuroses.

24 September-
3 October: + Usually, lively and sociable. Seeks for harmonious cooperation and emotional (sexual) fulfillment.

— There may be a likelihood of some vacillation or instability in love-attachments. Difficult relationships would tend to give rise to agitation, irritability, sexual problems. Possibly, an increased likelihood of hypersensitive response in those born close to the 28th and 29th.

4-13 October: + Sociable, though often prefers to maintain a sense of independence. Self-esteem may be apparent, and may incline to a reformistic attitude. Strives to overcome (or avoid) obstacles and achieve recognition/success.

— Self-willed, and can be prone to nervous tension. Difficulties in relationships could lead to irritability, mood swings, rebelliousness. Those born near to the 9th may be more likely to manifest hypertensive conditions.

14-23 October: + Usually, sociable and cooperative. Seeks to understand and be understood. Affectionate and sympathetic towards others. Can be imaginative.

— Possibly over-idealistic in love matters, and may be prone to nervous/emotional troubles arising from difficulty in relationships or disappointments.

24 October-   + Tenacious in pursuing selected objectives.
2 November: Intensity of feelings, probably which it is felt must be kept under control. Seeks for deep, emotional fulfillment. May desire excitement and stimuli (including sexual).

— The inclination to obstinacy and self-will may give rise, under pressure, to emotional disturbances, perhaps tending towards obsessiveness. Undue repression of the strong inner drives/urges could give rise to mood swings, irritability, agitation, sexual neuroses.

3-12 November: + Usually has an instinctive, intuitive understanding, and can be particularly prone to emotional stimuli. May be attracted to anything that provides excitement, erotic or otherwise. In some instances, might like to be regarded as a mysterious or interesting personality.

— Often imaginative, and if this quality is over-active it could lead to self-deception, lack of clarity in viewing the motives of others. Those born near to the 3rd could be more inclined to nervous sensitivity. Those born near to the 9th may sometimes incline to over-reaction, hyper-response.

13-22 November: + Often feels the need to actively strive. Seeks to direct and control—self and/or others. Can be motivated by deep, emotional drives. May desire success and stimulation. Usually has a capacity for tenacious persistence.

— Anxiety and stress could arise from frustration and disappointments in not achieving what is felt to be expected. Over-conscientiousness could lead to circumspect behaviour, perhaps depression. Desires security and freedom from worries.

23 November-
2 December: + Imaginative, idealistic, and often something of an optimist. Has a capacity for enjoying social involvement.

— May be over-imaginative, which could give rise to absent-mindedness and lack of foresight. In some cases this might show as negligence, because of the possible dislike for detail.
    Those born close to the 28th and 29th could be more inclined to anxieties.

3-12 December: + Mobile, with enthusiastic assertion of personal convictions. May seek for satisfaction in social (and sexual) relationships.

— Susceptible to stimuli—may become rather

over-excitable. Disappointments could produce feelings of inadequacy, loss of determination, perhaps sexual inhibitions.

Those born near to the 9th and 10th may be prone to psychosomatic troubles.

13-22 December: + Usually, self-determining and enthusiastic in tackling obstacles in order to achieve popularity, and/or success. Seeks for stimuli.

— Frustrations and disappointments may result in anxiety as there could be a sensitiveness to stress conditions or restrictions. Becomes impatient, irritable and hypertensive. Nervous conditions or hypersensitivity may be more apparent in those born close to the 17th.

23-31 December: + Usually restrained and patiently industrious in seeking to attain security. There is often an ability to concentrate efforts in the gaining of long-term objectives.

— There may be a possibility of over-conscientiousness. Goals may be too narrowly defined, and pursued at the expense of broader considerations. Could tend to one-sidedness and obstinacy. Therefore, might tend to obsessiveness. Tends to anxiety in the pursuit of material security, and could be vulnerable to depression. Uncertainty and/or loneliness may give rise to assumed indifference.

Note: Although the above list has been checked and tested by senior clinicians, including a professor of psychology, members of the social services, and a wide range of the general public, and appears to have a reasonably high level of relevancy, it remains, of necessity, a generalization, derived from the fundamental principles involved in the sun's annual cycle.

3. SELF-HELP

Dr H. Guntrip, an eminent psychiatrist, has observed that there is a widespread need for therapy among people 'who do not take their need to any doctor, and who would not get help if they did' (see bibliography). Of course, he was referring to the more severe conditions of neuroses that can be relieved by psychotherapy, but it was his observation that prompted me, as much as anything, to investigate self-analysis and self-help, at least for the more common states of mild anxiety and stress, and to find out whether astrology could assist, even if only upon the basis of a broad-spectrum analysis.

Stress in the Modern World

Mild conditions of stress, so commonly experienced by most of us these days, is not something that the majority of us immediately seek medical advice or treatment for; yet stress can still be a nagging, worrisome thing, hovering in the background of our daily lives and blunting the keen edge to our enjoyment of life.

The readily available palliatives, alcohol and tobacco, are not finally helpful, and can damage the health if they are taken in excess. Food is often resorted to as a comforter, but too much of this can bring its own problems. Incidentally, have you noticed the proliferation of books, articles and television programmes on the culinary arts? Is this another sign of the underlying stresses within society today? It is true, too, that the consumption of tranquillizers has reached staggering proportions—something like 18 million tablets prescribed in the U.K. during 1976, and an increase to 25 million by 1977! But tranquillizers do not treat the cause, only the symptoms, so it makes sense to try and make an attempt to get at the root of the matter for ourselves.

Susceptibility to Stress

There is evidence to support the idea that some types of personality are more prone to stress than others, though, as you can imagine, there are so many variables in human nature, and such a variety of environmental conditions, that it is almost impossible for researchers to claim one hundred per cent certainty in such matters. It is evident to most of us, for example, that living in a town or large city imposes far greater stresses than living in the quiet of the country—if indeed there is still such a thing in this age of factory farming and jet airliners!

But whether we feel particularly vulnerable, extra sensitive to conditions around us, and liable to tense up quicker than we feel is normal (if one could ever define what is 'normal'), there are a number of definite steps we can take to either correct or alleviate stress conditions. Although the first section of this chapter deals with relaxation and the simple routine for achieving this, it is important to give equal attention to the other sections as well. It is hoped that any particular suggestions that appeal to you will be selected and formed into a daily routine. So, determine now to work out a regular, daily routine of positive actions that will all combine to promote that sense of buoyancy and well-being that you so much desire to regain. It is no good just saying to yourself that such and such looks like a good idea, and that you will try it when you have a moment. It will be far more effective if you construct a set plan, on paper, with the intention of keeping to that plan for a week, a month, or however long you want—but do give yourself a fair chance.

If you have had some degree of tension for a long time, you are not going to shrug it off over night just because you've made a passing attempt at the relaxation exercise. More than likely you have had a good deal of practice at tensing-up, so you will need a fair amount of practice at unwinding, although you will have nature on your side, for the body is forever ready to restore the balance, if you give it half a chance. Try keeping a daily record in a simple note-book. You can revise your schedule as you go along, if you want to, and at the end of each month, say, you can comment on your progress, such as 'feeling much easier, and more relaxed when the boss calls me into his office', or 'don't get so knotted-up when I go for interviews'.

Relaxation

One of the off-shoots of continual tension is high blood pressure, and Professor H. Benson (see bibliography), has observed that one of the most significant factors in causing this is 'the necessity to cope with an environment requiring continuous behavioural adjustment'. Few are so fortunate today that they can entirely escape the echoes of world conflicts which are continually pumped into our homes. One way or another, the majority of us need to consider more and more the importance of counterbalancing the almost inescapable stresses within society itself. However, whether the stresses appear to come from within or without, let us make a start at lessening our own tensions.

Muscular Awareness

What you require, first of all, is an increased awareness of your muscular system and the particular areas that seem to be most prone to tension. For example, if you are sitting fairly upright while reading this, observe whether your shoulders are slightly raised or hunched. Would they be in a more relaxed position if they were dropped? And what of your jaw muscles? Are your teeth clenched without your realizing it?

The back of the neck is also vulnerable to tension. Try holding your chin down in its normal position and tightening up the muscles at the back of the neck, at the same time. You will find that a tremor develops. If you are an observant watcher of television you will have noticed that when someone is being interviewed and is nervous, exactly the same slight movement is noticeable. It takes quite an effort to contract the neck muscles sufficiently to produce that shaking, so just imagine the amount of nervous energy that is present.

Perhaps the most commonly effected muscles are those of the stomach, just below the breast-bone. Even a very slight, unconscious tensing here can produce an alteration of feeling, and subsequently, of mood. There is, incidentally, a most interesting astrological correlation between the stomach and the sign of Cancer, which is, in one of its aspects, considered to be the seat of the emotions. The solar plexus also lies in this area, and as its name implies, is, literally, a sun network or complex. Physically, of course, it is a main complex of nerves that meet in this region. By tradition, the sun is representative of the life force, self-expression and vitality, so here we have, both symbolically and in actuality, a highly significant juxtaposition, whether one chooses to view it in astrological or physiological terms.

It is evident enough through common experience that we feel and respond very distinctly 'in the pit of the stomach'. Who has not heard such expressions as, 'I've got a gut feeling', 'butterflies in my tummy', or, 'I'm all knotted up inside'. That sinking feeling before taking an examination or having to get up before an audience starts there, in the solar plexus region. If you are currently a little bit worried about something, place your hand over that area now. Can you identify it as the place where your feelings of unease appear to arise from?

Well, there is something you can do about that, but because I do not want you to take the idea of a relaxation routine in a too matter-of-fact way, let's coin a term or two for your first step towards easement of tension. How about 'Realistic Relaxation', or, 'Tranquility Time', or maybe, 'Floating Free Time'. Or think up something along those lines, for yourself. Something that conveys to you a pleasant period for your relaxation practice. This can become an entry in your note-book, reminding you of something to look forward to each day. You should set aside ten to twenty minutes, once or twice a day, though try to avoid a session for two hours after a meal.

Relaxation Technique

Find a quiet place, and a comfortable, upright chair to sit in. The posture to adopt is best described by visualizing those statues of Egyptian kings and queens. The back is straight and the head erect, with the shoulders dropped comfortably to the sides—not slouched forwards—and the forearms resting along the thighs; and hands are open and fingers just reaching over the knees. The thighs are at right-angles to the pelvis, and the knees are also bent at right-angles. In this position the weight of the head is taken squarely upon the spine, the arms are supported by the thighs, and the whole body rests comfortably, with a minimum use of energy or muscular effort. The reason for sitting rather than lying down on a comfortable bed or settee is because you would become so relaxed that there is a likelihood of dropping off to sleep, and this is not the aim. What is required is a positive awareness of relaxation, so that eventually you can achieve freedom from excess tension, or switch on an attitude of calm tranquility just be telling yourself to respond accordingly.

When you have selected a convenient place and are satisfied that you are sitting as comfortably as possible, close your eyes and endeavour to relax completely. Do this by first tensing up each muscle—go through the motions of stretching and yawning, if you like. Resume the posture, as described, and then direct the attention to each part of the body in turn, starting with the feet and telling yourself that they are completely relaxed, and then moving on to the legs, thighs, arms, back, neck, face and jaw muscles. Attend to each part in turn, and finish with the solar plexus region, where you might imagine, for instance, that there is a warm, comforting glow, radiating calmness and tranquility. There is no need to persist too long with this; just aim to relax and enjoy the experience as much as possible.

Having done that, the next thing to do is introduce a regular rhythm of breathing. The advantage in doing this is that it helps correct the iregularities in the easy flow of the life-force or vitality brought about by tension. Also, it aids relaxation. You may have noticed that when someone is asleep the breathing is slightly deeper and usually very regular. Try to simulate this, nice and easy, with the air taken in through the nostrils and directed towards the back of the throat, just as when one is about to start snoring, but not quite.

It will be found helpful to repeat a word to yourself, on the out-going breath, as a means for maintaining a constant rhythm. In eastern religions the word used as an aid to meditation is 'OM' (pronounced 'home'). You could equally well use 'Calm', or, as Professor Benson suggests, 'One' (see bibliography).

If distracting thoughts keep entering your mind, do not be concerned by them. Just accept them, and continue repeating the word you have chosen. Before long you should come to enjoy this practice. Even if you are one of those people who wake up tired after a night's sleep, you will be surprised at how refreshed one can feel after a little practice in this relaxation technique.

Bearing in mind that the main aim here is to establish a regular routine of practice, there is a refinement that could be introduced later on. For those who are constantly having to cope with stress-making situations the state of relaxation, once attained, can be used for post-hypnotic suggestion. For this you will need a key-word or phrase of your own devising which can act like a trigger or reminder, when you want to reinforce the relaxation. While sitting in the deeply relaxed condition, tell yourself that whenever you repeat such and such a word—whatever it is you choose—you will experience a glow of confidence, calm, peace, etc. Keep it simple, practice regularly, with patience, and gradually the unconscious will become permeated with this new thought, until, one day, when you least expect it, you will find yourself confidentally tackling difficult situations with a minimum amount of stress. Obviously, it is not to be expected that every scrap of tension should be removed, or we would end up like rag-dolls!

Diet

Initially, I suggested that it is best not to practice the relaxation exercise until two hours after a meal. There is a connection between the digestion of food and the ability to relax easily. If you are not completely convinced of this, just consider a fact that is well known to the medical and nursing profession. Elderly people can become very restless and have disturbed nights when suffering from constipation. When this is corrected they get to sleep more readily. Naturally, this is hardly noticeable in younger, active people, but isn't it worth taking just a little trouble over your diet if it can help you with your relaxation programme?

There is no need to become a food faddist, but a few sensible adjustments, as necessary, will do no harm, and indeed should prove a definite advantage in improving your general well-being. There is no need to take harmful laxatives. Just increase the amount of roughage in the diet by sprinkling a little bran on your food every day. (A book on bran is listed in the bibliography.) Wholemeal bread, fruit and vegetables are also good suppliers of roughage.

It makes sense, too, to reduce stimulants like tea, coffee and sugar. There is no need to cut these things out entirely: just reduce the intake of sugar, and drink your particular beverage weaker than you may have become accustomed to. Incidentally, alcohol is not a stimulant but a depressant, though tobacco is quite a strong stimulant which increases the blood-sugar, making the mind over-active and increasing restlessness and agitation, if there happens to be a tendency that way. Because it is also a vaso-constrictor—constricting the fine blood vessels just below the surface of the skin —it can increase blood-pressure and make the hands and feet feel cold, thus, producing in some people the very same symptoms as anxiety and tension!

As was observed earlier on, the basis of stress is fear. Fear begets tension which produces symptoms, which in turn produce more fear, more tension, and so on. This, of course, is the vicious circle I referred to in Chapter Two. It is something we want to break, not add fuel to. If you are suffering symptoms of stress, why not think again, if you happen to be a smoker?

Tissue Salts

With each of the short sun sign interpretations you will see that I have given the corresponding tissue salt. These are mineral salts, usually made into small tablets, at homoeopathic strength, and therefore quite safe. Their function is nutritional rather than medicinal, and it has been suggested by Vanda Sawtell (see bibliography) that there appears to be a correlation between the twelve tissue salts and the sun signs. The theory is that we all tend to burn up more of the salt common to our sign, and that, therefore, it could be of benefit to health to correct the imbalance with the appropriate salt.

The tissue salt that is specifically remommended for stress through worry or excitement is Kali Phos. (potassium phosphate), a deficiency of which, according to Dr J. B. Chapman, produces depression, fearfulness, etc. The astrological correlative to this salt is the sign Aries, symbolic of courage, self-determination, and everything, in fact, that is in counterpoint to anxiety and fear. Tissue salts are obtainable from health food shops, and from many chemists.

Self-realization

The term self-realization has many connotations, and can be seen as a natural process of being and becoming, at various levels of experience. An urge to discover the self, as in self-analysis, usually indicates the conscious attempt to further the process of awareness and integration. The reason why we should be considering self-realization at all is because it involves acceptance, and in this lies another clue in the search for greater peace of mind.

During relaxation practice you will become aquainted with one form of acceptance. This is in coming to realize that although anxieties and tensions produce various physical discomforts (or symptoms), it is possible for one to consciously accept the fact that the 'I' can stand aside, as it were, and call the tune. Thus, in the self-induced state of deep relaxation it becomes possible for one to consciously accept the fact that the body does not have to be continually on guard and keyed-up for action.

Realization and acceptance go together, while relaxation makes these things easier to accomplish. In order to make this clearer to you, here is a little test that you can apply for yourself.

First of all, think of someone who you find particularly irritating, annoying, or worrying in one way or another. Now, write down all those things about that person that you dislike so much. Then consider, if possible, why you should be worried or annoyed by such mannerisms. Lastly, carefully holding the list of dislikes in your mind, transfer them to yourself, and, with honesty, ask yourself if you are not harbouring any of those traits in yourself. You may well be surprised at the answers you get!

The truth is that we all unconsciously project parts of our personalities onto others, especially those parts we find it difficult to accept in ourselves. For example, if you feel unduly disturbed by assertive behaviour in someone else, it is very likely because you have an assertiveness within yourself that perhaps you had not realized. Or if you are an individual who despises an indecisive, weak-kneed attitude in others, think twice before making similar judgements in the future!

Acceptance of one's own faults and weaknesses is not always an easy thing to do, but it is a sure step on the way to improvement. It assures greater tolerance, not only of ourselves but of others. We have only to look about us to find that much of the world's ills are due to international tensions, exacerbated by intolerance.

In the section on using the list, the examples given showed that it was possible to gain a deeper insight into an individual's underlying motivations. This, of course, is another aspect of realization. When we are occcupied in situations that are not in accord with our true natures, then stress is almost inevitable. Let me enlarge upon this by giving you another example.

Some years ago, a senior member of the staff of a university, whom I shall call Robert, came to see me with a problem that he hoped could be resolved with the help of astrological analysis. He had been employed in a responsible position for some time. He liked the work, and the surroundings were quiet and extremely pleasant. And yet, for no apparent reason, he had been experiencing bouts of weakness and panicky attacks for some months, and feared that he might actually faint. When I questioned Robert about his background he told me that his parents had impressed upon him the need to work for a high level of academic ability. Being a dutiful son, he struggled to obtain a good degree, and having accomplished this it seemed to be but a natural progression to continue in the academic life.

It will convey to you some idea of his feelings of desperation when I tell you that he travelled almost three hundred miles to talk to me about his condition, which was so clearly one of severe anxiety and stress. Now, you may well be puzzled as to why Robert should suffer in the way he did, when, as we have seen, he was an intelligent man, in an occupation he was well qualified to deal with, and in surroundings to be envied by many. Analysis of his chart presented a clear picture of the personality structure and patterns, and it was not difficult to see that Robert was in a career entirely unsuited to his true personality. From the analysis it was possible to indicate all the various potentials and type of orientation most agreeable to the inner, and up until that time, unconscious nature. The observations made from the chart were later fully confirmed by Robert, after he had visited London for two lengthy sessions of psychological testing by specialists in career aptitudes.

As soon as Robert came to realize that adjustments would have to be made in his career life the anxiety and tension faded away. The simple fact of realizing, through increased awareness of himself, that what he had been doing was something that had been expected of him *by others,* and not something that was more in harmony with his own centre of being, was sufficient to ease away all the doubts and uncertainties that had been repressed because of a sense of guilt in daring to consider other fields of endeavour that, perhaps, he believed his parents would not have approved of.

Although Robert's chart produced all the detailed information necessary to make the required deductions, it is of interest to see how the much simpler sun sign interpretation of tendencies might have been applied in this case. Robert was born on 17 August, in the sign of Leo, and from that alone we might deduce, for example, that there might be a love of gambling and entertainment, confidence, organizing ability, and all those traits that are associated with Leo in popular astrology. Clearly, that would not tell us a great deal about the problem; and in fact, Robert's outward personality appeared to have little in common with the popular concepts, being (seemingly) quiet, studious, and introspective, and nothing like the 'self-confident, fun-loving Leonian' of journalistic parlance.

However, if we now refer to the list we find that although Robert should be active and enterprising, in a Leonian way, there is a need, too, to seek recognition, security and good relationships. Our very first and most significant relationship is the parental one, and as young children we are liable to do anything to hold the love and affection of our parents. Unfortunately, parents sometimes indulge in moral blackmail. Pressures of this kind usually mean that somewhere along the way we have to modify our personalities to an extent that is far removed from our true natures, and so the foundations of later stress are laid.

Although in his mid-thirties, Robert was unmarried, and though this was not an area of his life that we discussed, it is evident from reference to the list that relationship matters are of significance. And, of course, recognition and security, whether sought for in the parents, or otherwise, would have helped to keep Robert pursuing a particular course, perhaps in the face of what his inner voice was trying to tell him.

Accepting and Understanding Stress

In this illustration we have another clue to the answer. Self-help should mean, for you, a firm resolve to simply understand your particular stresses, and *not* to blindly struggle to overcome them. The list should provide a starting point for you in the search for greater equanimity. Minor anxieties and stresses, such as we are dealing with here, can usually be considerably eased by a few simple measures, as in aquiring the relaxation technique, and trying, if necessary, to gain a fresh perspective upon the true nature of the self. It could be, however, that with growing awareness of one's own, unique potentials, there comes a time when some sort of alteration in the life-style might become a consideration. For example, a job that pays less money might be preferable to a well-paid one that entails frustrations or tensions which you are not fully prepared to accept. Realization should mean both the acceptance of one's weaknesses, as well as the growing recognition of one's true nature and potential.

The fact that acceptance, not only of external realities but inner tensions too, is of much importance to any consideration of the stress problem can be seen in the observations of a woman patient who wrote to C. G. Jung, saying that: 'I always thought that when we accepted things they overpowered us in some way or other. This turns out not to be true at all, and it is only by accepting them that one can assume an attitude towards them.' This apparently simple observation, born out of hard experience, contains so much insight and wisdom that it is well worth reflecting upon.

Acceptance is not easy, and never has been. Pride, for example, is like a veneer of polish over the fragile personality that finds in others what it dare not see in itself; hate is a superficial expression of dislike that reflects deeper feelings of self-depreciation. As we have seen, there is a tendency for all human beings to project upon others the very things that they cannot accept in themselves. Our fears become transferred to people or objects about us. Dr Clair Weekes talking about agoraphobia (fear of open places), says it 'is really only another face of anxiety'. And she goes on to explain that the cure is found in the places that you avoid—you can not run away from yourself—and that acceptance of the panic feeling is the answer.

In the self-induced state of calm and relaxation it is often possible to reflect quietly upon one's circumstances, and to try and recall an episode in the past that could have been the cause for the present sense of anxiety or tension. Sometimes, upon realization of the truth, it is as though there is a sudden flash of understanding that brings with it a sense of immense relief. Even just finding out, like Robert, that we have been forcing ourselves to behave in a pattern foreign to our nature, can appear to work like a miracle.

Of course, it is not always easy to delve into memories of the past, and when the original experience has been particularly traumatic it may well have been blocked-off from consciousness. This really brings us into the province of more severe conditions that require a trained analyst's assistance in explaining the links between past episodes and present symptoms of discomfort, though a brief comment here may be of general interest. I think that Dr Culver M. Barker sums it up very well in his term 'the point of critical hurt'. This, he suggests, may be seen through the suspended personalities of childhood or teens, as found in dream material. Through the insights gained by dream analysis the therapist enables the patient to identify 'positively and constructively' with the forgotten traumatic phase, in the form of what Dr Barker calls 'feedback', and the healing process takes place.

Thus, and this is certainly true in most mild conditions of stress, there is everything to gain in practising constructive self-analysis, in order to bring about realization and acceptance. If it seems that I keep returning to the idea of acceptance, it is for the very good reason that this is fundamental to the practice of self-help. Indeed,

Dr Clair Weekes, in describing self-treatment for 'nerves', emphasizes true acceptance of the physical condition. She says: 'Let float and not fight.' This sentiment has its equivalent in religious philosophy, where the thought is expressed in, 'Let go. Let God.'

Religion

Some readers may wonder why I have included religion as a topic for consideration in our approach to self-help in stress. I think this can be answered right away by giving you C. G. Jung's comment about the woman patient's views concerning acceptance. You will recall that she said that through acceptance she found it possible to assume an attitude. In other words, acceptance of apparently overwhelming feelings actually released her from the emotional bonds that she had suffered previously and had tried to run away from. Jung observed that, 'This attitude is religious in the truest sense, and therefore therapeutic, for all religions are the therapies for the sorrows and disorders of the soul.'

Incidentally, you will find several references to Jung throughout this book. To many, he is considered to be one of the outstanding pioneers of modern psychology, whose contributions to our understanding of the psyche has been far greater than was previously realized. His clear insight into the structures of personality have also added to the sum total of astrological knowledge, as we shall see in the next chapter.

People have a variety of ideas about a God, depending upon their religious upbringing, or lack of it; but for the majority of us, some sort of belief in an overall Godhead, no matter how shaky our views may be, serves as a comfort and support in times of need. Even the atheist has been known to exlcaim, 'Oh, my God!' in a moment of crisis! In his investigations of the unconscious mind, Jung found that it actually contains two levels, personal and impersonal. Just below the surface of consciousness lie all the impressions and memories of the past in what Jung termed the 'personal unconscious'. Below that again lies the 'collective unconscious', a mysterious area in which are contained hereditary memories and race images of a primal nature: fire, sea-monsters, demons, sun, moon, animals, the hero figure, earth mother, Self, or God, etc. All these images, and many more, can be found in the myths and legends of our entire civilization, but—and here is the interesting thing—they sometimes reveal themselves in dreams.

When the conscious ego, the little 'I', is pursuing a course of action that is not in tune with the self as a whole, the unconscious starts sending up messages from the deeper levels of the 'collective unconscious' in the form of primal images. These take shape, usually in dreams, and to these dream symbols Jung gave the name 'archetypes'. The message that the unconscious is sending up is usually one that is telling us how to correct what is wrong, if we can but interpret the dream symbolism. Nature is continually restoring the balance, and this is no less true for human beings than it is for anything else on God's earth.

The collective unconscious of an individual may be seen as a gateway to the vast experiences of one's racial and universal heritage throughout the course of time. The scientist, I suppose, might observe this as our link with the 'time-space continuum'. It is as though, if we are able to reach deep within ourselves, through the dark and mysterious recesses of the mind, there comes a point at which awareness—if that is the right word—extends to something beyond, and greater than ourselves. You can see where this idea leads us? It stems from Jung's reasoning, the reasoning of the scientific mind, but it is no latter day revelation, for the pursuit of greater insight into self—self-realization—leading on to an awareness of 'Self', the unity of one with the 'Whole', is at the heart of all great religions, and probably best known in the meditational practices evolved in the East.

Most students of Yoga, now very popular in the Western world, know that purposeful meditation, while in the relaxed state (similar to that described), soon achieves an extension of awareness, and that a great sense of peace can be experienced that is attributed to the realization of 'Atman' or 'The One'. This very same idea is to be found in Christianity, of course, and is well defined in such mystical books as *The Cloud of Unknowing.*

Astrologers have little difficulty in recognizing the existence of a sort of cosmic link between self and 'Self', or, to put it another way, in being able to perceive a Divine Order behind the chaos and complexities of our little lives, here upon earth. Every birth chart (horoscope) captures a planetary pattern in a fleeting moment in time, and every pattern reflects the impress of a circuit within the psyche. Psychologists, like Jung, are aware that we hold, deep in the unconscious, an instinctive awareness of an overall self, whether it is expressed as Self, or in religious terms, as God.

The cleric would affirm that the Lord created man in His own image. Religion encourages a faith in an Eternal God, and thus provides a continual support; but more than that, it demonstrates the powerful and creative force of Love. We are all familiar with the First and Second Commandments, and it is not my intention to preach but to suggest that the giving of love to others can be, in itself, a greater healer to the troubled spirit. In the light of what we have seen about unwittingly projecting onto others the very things we hate in ourselves, the words of the Second Commandment, which commends us to love our neighbours as ourselves, are revealed as being full of insight and wisdom.

Naturally, not everyone will want to avail themselves of religious support, but anyone who is interested may like to know of a little book that is a real gem. Called *The Practice of the Presence of God,* it was written by a Brother Lawrence of the barefooted Carmelite order, in the seventeenth century. A humble and unlettered young man, he did his best to follow the religious doctrine, but found it a great struggle. Instead, he went right to the heart of the matter and started imagining that God was with him all the time. This simple practice helped him so greatly that gradually a wonderful sense of joy and love developed, and this continued to support him in peace and tranquillity throughout his life. His message is simple, his method so uncomplicated; but they give evidence of results that can be highly beneficial, for, as we are told elsewhere, 'There is no fear in love, but perfect love casteth our fear.'

Of course, Christianity does not have a priority on the theme of love. Let me give you the words of the Indian saint, Shri Dada. He taught Adyatma Yoga, which embraces Adwaita, the philosophy of non-duality, in which it is seen that the inner self of man is identical with the supreme Reality (Brahman). 'To have peace you must give peace to those with whom you come into contact.' He goes on to say, 'It is useless to retire from the world; we take our ego with us. If you cannot see peace in the battle of life itself, you have not understood the truth.'

My own sentiments, for what they are worth, are contained in the following:

> Find God in a flower
> And he is in your heart.
> Listen to God on the wind,
> For he is all about.
> See God in the stars, and
> You and He are One.

Recreation and Balance

The idea that there should be a reasonable balance between work and leisure is obvious enough, though the full significance of the role which pastime activities play in our development is often overlooked. In all of nature stresses occur when one thing is pursued at the expense of another, or, conversely, when there is neglect of any part. The inherent response to imbalance is to compensate, in order to restore equilibrium. If we have not been guided in recreation (recreation) or have neglected that part of our lives, the consequences may not be immediately obvious, but are just as far-reaching.

This can be graphically illustrated by visualizing the wheel of the Zodiac with its twelve signs, each counterbalancing its opposite number. Aries-Libra, for example, referring to the interplay between 'I' and 'You', or Cancer-Capricorn, with their implication of reciprocal action between home and work life. Leo is the sign traditionally related to pastimes, pleasures, and, most significantly, self-expression. It reflects that essential phase of life in which a child discovers its individual potentials through play, and in which too, as we mature, continual affirmation of self is accomplished—as and when necessary—through the development of talents, gifts, and personal creativity.

Leo's opposite sign is Aquarius, symbolic of the group, as in societies, movements, causes, organizations. At the personal level it relates to the natural desire to become more than we are, to transform or transcend ourselves. In the normal course of events we pursue a hobby or talent until such time as we feel a need to share our interest with others, perhaps by joining a club. Or, we have a pastime which affords us much pleasure, and we find that we can improve and extend our interest only through participation with others. Either way, the Leo-Aquarius interplay is fulfilled in a happy, equable manner. But what happens when the Leonian factor in the life-pattern is neglected? The individual cannot adequately express him or herself in a personally fulfilling way, and seeks satisfaction in areas other than those which draw forth the individual's creative expression. For a youngster, so thwarted, attraction can lie in simply going along with the crowd, where perhaps, the urge to be different (Aquarius) is pandered to at the expense of development as an individual (Leo). Note, for example, the cult of the 'way-out' pop group, where the emphasis is upon being different, and the expression upon the faces of many of the young people involved is joyless—the opposite of Leonian gaiety and fun.

The more neglected the Leonian factor, the greater likelihood of over-compensation via the Aquarian factor. The sad irony is that a youngster who, for whatever reason, bypasses the Leonian phase of development and adopts without question the standards and uniform of a collective movement falls into a trap of self-delusion. The adopted style and mannerisms of the group perhaps provide temporary compensation; but without that sense of true individuality so essential for balanced expression of self, frustrations and uncertainties will flourish like rampant weeds within the psyche, flowering forth into anger and rebelliousness. And so creative and constructive expression becomes destructive.

Echoes of a Leo-Aquarian unbalance are all too evident in today's society, where the movement is towards ever-increasing business monopolies and multi-national enterprises; where words like state-control, commune, co-operative and collective dissemi-nate throughout the 'mass media', and television resides resplendent, the arch-Aquarian symbol of them all! Today, more than ever before, there is every benefit in considering your own creative interests as a counter to stresses, not only of the daily grind, but also to the increasing pressures that a modern society imposes upon us.

This is common sense, when you come to think about it; but the trouble is, that when we are so embroiled in our own problems, distracted by emotions and events, thinking ceases to be quite as helpful as it might be. The ego, caught up in anxieties and tensions, loses sight of the self as a whole, and needs re-creative activity to restore the balance. Becoming involved in a pleasurable hobby, sport or other pastime, serves to correct this fine balance. When we are completely absorbed in doing something we enjoy doing, self-consciousness ceases to exist, and for a little while we merge into a blissful state of being and fulfilling. But more than that, recreation provides the vehicle of communication through which we, in however a modest or grandiose way, may express ourselves to the world at large.

Do not dismiss leisure activity with the excuse that you just do not have the time or the energy. If you have time to be over-concerned or worried about yourself, you have time for an alternative interest! Moreover, pleasurable activity and exercise actually release energy, as well as encouraging muscular relaxation. Even such simple pastimes as walking and gardening impart a sense of well-being to the jaded soul.

One man who derived a great deal of benefit from taking up a hobby was Sir Winston Churchill. He started painting in his middle years, at a time when the burdens of political life lay heavy upon his shoulders. If you feel you could get pleasure from paint-brush and palette, start right in, but be quite sure that this form of art is for you. In an age of package-deals, commercialism and television, it is all to easy to fall for something that everyone else appears to be enjoying. Not so long ago, for instance, small fortunes were spent on skate-board and jogging equipment, by many people who afterwards found that these sporting activities did not adequately fulfill their individual needs. To some extent, television has usurped individual ingenuity and time and we must all be aware of this subtle infringement upon our self-expression. Does this sound like the home-spun philosophy of a Will Rogers? Well, even if it does, maybe there is something to be said for getting back to the days of the porch, the pocket-knife and a good piece of wood to whittle!

Genuine Self-expression

The point is, that although we may be swayed by mass communication and group influences, so long as we are aware of the fact, we can do something about it—by making very sure that what we elect to do as individuals arises from our natures, our heredity and our upbringing, and not from some passing fancy that happens to be promoted by the media. Get hold of that deep inner urge to do something, make something that is uniquely you, that expresses your feelings and releases hidden springs of creativity or vitality. This is the way that personal emotions which cannot be externalized in any other way, find expression.

Generally speaking, the arts provide a good channel for emotional energy, but activated and pent-up feelings also translate into physical energy and so some form of exercise should not be overlooked. (Students of astrology will be aware of the interplay of opposites here, as symbolized by the pair, Mars-Venus.) A good compromise is an art that entails some extra physical exertion, like woodcarving, sculpting, dancing. There is something to be said, after all, for the good old art of whittling!

The sun signs divide naturally into four categories that come reasonably close to main personality tendencies. These may provide you with a general guideline to appropriate types of leisure activity:

Aries, Leo,
Sagittarius:

Normally, active, self-motivating, mobile. Need outlets for physical and emotional drives. Relaxation through rhythmic exertion. e.g., sports.

Taurus, Virgo,
Capricorn:

Normally, practical, stable, structuring. Need outlets providing scope for constructive application of abilities. Relaxation through rhythmic, industrious productivity. e.g., crafts.

Gemini, Libra,
Aquarius:

Normally, versatile and mentally alert. Need intellectual stimuli and social communication. Relaxation through harmonious exchange. e.g., intellectual and artistic interests.

Cancer, Scorpio,   Normally, receptive, responsive, intuitive.
Pisces: Need channels for externalizing inner im-
                           pressions and feelings. Relaxation through
                           harmonious expression of emotional drives.
                           e.g., art and exercise.

Letting Off Steam

A great deal of suffering and tension arises out of repressed anger or
aggressiveness, especially among women, in whom such things are
not always recognized because it is not considered 'lady-like' or
proper to vent such feelings too vigorously. If an individual, of
either sex, is naturally aggressive or assertive, too strong a
supression will eventually result in stress feelings. The sun sign
lists will more than likely give you an indication of your true
nature, and if you are able to decide that such considerations do
apply, there is plenty you can do. Even the simple fact of
acknowledging one's own aggression helps to lessen the pressure.
If you have not been taking any exercise, start in on some form of
physical activity right away.

I have heard it suggested that one can let off steam very well by
beating the daylights out of an old pillow, so why not fling yourself
on the bed and pound away! Scream and shout too, if it is not going
to disturb the neighbours. I rather like the story about a leading
musician who had a violent temper. His colleagues suffered, his
family suffered, and so did he. One day he came home in a particularly vile mood, saw a flower-pot, picked it up and threw it with all
his might against the garden wall. It smashed to pieces in such a
delightfully satisfying way that he looked around for another
flower-pot and tried again. When he eventually got indoors he
found that his temper had evaporated. Thereafter, he always kept a
good supply of flower-pots handy, and he and everyone were a lot
happier.

Summary

In this chapter we have looked at four aspects, each capable of being instrumental in easing tensions. You may well think of other alternatives, and if so, work them into your routine. However, I believe these four do cover the main areas of experience. They are the ones that crop up time and again, in various guises, wherever and whenever the 'human condition' has come under consideration. **Relaxation,** and techniques for acquiring it, have been diligently pursued for health and religious purposes from the earliest times. **Realization,** a philosophical concept that is well summed up in the words of the ancient Greek oracle 'Man, Know Thyself', reflects the inborn tendency in everyone of us to discover our inner selves in the process of becoming complete beings—to achieve 'individuation', as Jung said—and is clearly reflected in the sophisticated systems of astrology that have evolved in the course of some two and half thousand years. Understanding of self leads to acceptance, and this implies a double blessing, for we can only love our neighbours when we love ourselves.

Religions echo this philosophy and imbue it with a faith that enables us to transcend, from self to Self. 'Holiness', 'wholeness', or self-integration are different ways of expressing the same thing. Love of God is a unifying thing that brings harmony to the psyche or soul.

Recreation is an aspect of life that is sometimes overlooked in this hectic world of ours, where labour-saving appliances seem to only allow us time for pre-packed, electronic entertainment. But no matter how hesitant, modest or faltering is your little bit of art work or effort, it is a valuable palliative for daily tensions, and a recognized (psychologically) way towards unification of the self.

As suggested at the beginning of this chapter, do make a positive move to actually do something. Buy that note book or diary, and start jotting down the steps you want to build into the daily routine. Get the relaxation exercise established, along with any reasonable adjustment to diet that you think will be an advantage. Do not neglect some form of regular, rhythmic exercise, especially if you lead a sedentary life. This includes, deep, easy breathing, to a regular count, which has a useful calming effect.

If you feel it will help, review your life-style in the light of the guide-lines provided by the list. The feeling of a need to search your inner self is very often an indication of the commencement of the process of self-integration. It is always a challenge, though the choice of whether or not you are going to do anything about it is entirely your own. A religion provides us with support and additional (psychic) strength to meet the challenge. The serious student of astrology, perhaps more than most, stands in awe and reverence at the wonder of the universal patterns that seem to indicate the Divine Order of things. If one has any semblance of faith in a God, then the vividly graphic quality of an individual birth chart and the profundity of astrological symbolism is such as to reaffirm and reinforce one's beliefs a hundredfold.

This, of course, is just a personal view, but the point behind it is that if anyone who is suffering anxiety and stress feels, instinctively or intuitively, that the cause of the trouble is in the style of life, even though things seem to be going along very nicely on the surface, then it pays to use whatever means are to hand to discover the truth and gain the right perspective. Whenever a client or friend tells me that they are doing such-and-such, but *feel* they should be doing something else, the chances are that their birth chart will confirm their underlying feelings, for fulfillment comes only when we are operating on all levels.

In the remaining chapters I am going to tell you a little more about astrology and its link with personality. It has always seemed to me that a great deal has been written for students of astrology, that even more has been published on the popular sun signs, but that very little has been written about the subject itself for the general public. This is probably due to the very good reason that, like psychology or any other specialized subject, astrology has its own technical terminology. I think, however, that if we move out from the platform of the personality (psychology), first of all, there is a good chance that you will be able to follow the theme into the deeper though fascinating waters of astrological symbolism.

4. THE PSYCHOLOGY OF ASTROLOGY

Psychology, the study of the psyche, or soul, and mind, is a comparatively young science, although as a continuation of the age-old quest for self-knowledge its roots are merged in philosophy and theosophy. Astrology, arising directly out of the earliest astronomical observations, is possibly the oldest of sciences dealing with the study of personality and behaviour. Its evolution has, to some extent, kept pace with general understanding and advancement in the sciences, though it does tend to be held back at times, bogged down by its own technical ramifications and an out-moded phraseology that even today lingers on in a style of astrological jargon that you may have come across: 'Your romantic Venus is currently afflicted by disruptive Uranus in your house of love and luck . . .' It certainly means nothing to me, so I should be surprised if it really meant anything to the average reader with little or no knowledge of astrology.

It was C. G. Jung who, in his investigations of the far-reaches of the conscious and unconscious mind, discovered the all-pervasiveness of astrology. This is best described in his own comment, made while observing a painting done by a patient undergoing psychotherapy, in which a moon and stars could be seen. 'It is an allusion to the unconscious astrology which is in our bones, though we are unaware of it.'

Jung was a prolific writer and lecturer, though in the twenties and thirties his ideas were not readily understood or accepted, for the extent of his researches and the breadth of his vision far out-stripped that of his contemporaries—and this includes Freud, with his then popular, but limited, sex-orientated psychology. Because Jung's researches embraced the symbols of legend and myth throughout the course of civilization, he was able to present ideas about the working of the mind in a way which had not been possible before, although, in a curious way, while a great deal went over the heads of his scientific colleagues, much of what he said or wrote made very good sense to the more serious astrologers of the time.

Dane Rudhyar, an outstanding astrologer and writer, was one of those who did appreciate Jung's work, and he set about producing what is still one of the classics in modern astrological literature, *The Astrology of Personality,* which was first published in the autumn of 1936 in America. But if the average psychiatrist and psychoanalyst of those days had not realized the significant role that astrological symbolism plays in the lives of everyone, Jung had; for he would sometimes employ the services of astrologers in cases difficult to diagnose by other means.

Only in the last decade or so have psychologists begun fully to realize the importance of Jung's findings and the vast amount of wisdom to be found in his writings. In more recent times, too, astrology has advanced considerably, thanks to the painstaking work of scientists like Michel Gauquelin, psychologist and statistician, and Professor H. J. Eysenck, whose collaboration with Jeff Mayo, a leading author and teacher of astrology, produced a scientific paper (*The Journal of Social Psychology,* 1978, 220-236) of much value to the astrological world. It is of particular interest because it clearly shows the relationship between the attitudes of extraversion and introversion, as defined by Jung, with the sun signs. Their researches covered over 2000 subjects, and a study of the distribution of sun positions through the twelve signs shows a remarkable similarity with the traditionally observed alter-nation, between signs, from positive (extravertive) to negative (introvertive). Beneath the diagram of the horoscope on page 23 you will see a simple graph of the distribution, illustrating just how close is the correlation between the two personality traits and the month of birth. As a scientific paper it marks a particularly important milestone along the astrological path, for it encouraged the first ever astrological conference to be held at the Institute of Psychiatry in London in May 1979.

The Four Function Types

Besides defining the two broad categories of extraversion and introversion, Jung also observed and described what he termed the four function types: thinking, feeling, sensation and intuition. He suggested that if one function was used more than the others, this would be the superior function, while its opposite would be the inferior function. For example, if the thinking function is dominant in one's personality, then feeling is the neglected function, and vice versa. A person who thinks a great deal can often become worried by feelings, and a feeling person can be worried by thoughts. If one operates mainly via sensations—'Let's be sensible about this'—then intuition is the neglected function, and anything that cannot be explained in concrete terms, or arises unprompted into the mind, becomes a disturbing influence. An intuitive type, on the other hand, responds to the 'hunch', and the impressions that spring from the unconscious, and only feels irritated or restricted by the confines of reality and too much insistence upon common sense.

The two attitudes of introversion and extraversion can each be combined with the four function types to make eight variations, but it is as well to remember that all such attempts to define behaviour patterns or classify personality serve only to provide useful guidelines to better understanding. It is impossible to place people into neat little categories, no matter how scientific the approach may be. Jung himself was at pains to make this clear. However, in all these definitions you will have noticed that the law of opposites is present. Feeling types find it difficult to understand why thinking types do not respond with the same passion, and intuition types might not always understand why sensation types appear to be obsessed with material considerations or security.

When one function is over-worked, compensation must come from its opposite if balance is to be restored. Obviously, this is an over-simplification, but I am sure you will have grasped the general idea. In actuality, this swing from one function to another, and the struggle for balance, are part of a continual process within the personality and constitutes what Jung saw as the striving for integration and self-realization.

Male and Female Attributes

Jung found that the sun and moon—prominent in myth, legend and religion from the earliest times—are often given the attributes of male and female respectively: e.g., sun king, giver of life, symbol of fertility; or Diana, moon goddess, Luna, queen of the night, etc. In the full light of the sun we perceive clearly, and so the sun is synonymous with intellect, while the ethereal qualities of moon-light more fittingly reflect the mysterious nature of dreamland and the unconscious. In this we can readily see correlations between gender and thinking-feeling, conscious-unconscious, etc. In fact, the male-female factors play a significant part in the psychological make-up of every individual, and Jung identified them with the names animus and anima, which have their equivalent at the physical level—every male carries some undeveloped female characteristics, and vice versa. The result of a male or female hormone imbalance is very well known.

And so it is, that in any investigation of the individual psychology, the influence of the parents is closely examined via childhood memories and impressions. For example, if a young woman cannot easily relate to men, chances are that some early impression of the father (animus) is thwarting her natural tendencies. Likewise, a very masculine, 'he-man' type may have difficulty in accepting his anima, and so all females become objects for dominance and subjugation—remember what was said about how we tend to project those parts of our personalities onto others that we cannot accept in ourselves. In this respect, animus and anima play a major role.

Jung's explanation of the unconscious imagery or archetypes made it possible for psychoanalysts to approach the hidden depths of the mind with much greater understanding, and for astrologers, traditional symbolism which had, hitherto, been intuitively understood, now began to make sense. In short, Jung made psych-ological analysis of the birth chart (horoscope) possible, and astrology, as a science, took a leap forward. Your sun sign will tell you something about certain of your father's characteristics, but not all of them, because there are other features in a chart to be taken into account; but your moon's sign, if you know it and the 'house' position, will tell you quite a lot about your mother's disposition and her likely influence upon you as a child. ('House' refers to the twelve sectors of the birth chart.)

Astrology and Psychological Diagnosis

It is the relative ease with which one is able to construct an in-depth picture of personality and infer the likely orientation of it to the various areas of life experience that clearly makes the employment of astrological techniques in the field of psychology so worth while. Students of astrology have been aware of this for many years, but it is only in comparatively recent times that a more active interest has been taken by trained psychologists and psychiatrists. The fact that astrology can be of real assistance in clinical work has not been entirely overlooked, however. Perhaps the observations of a noteworthy American psychologist, R. Metzner (who took the trouble to learn chart calculation and interpretation before making any comment) may be of interest. He believes that astrology, as a means for psychological typing and making diagnoses, exceeds 'in complexity and sophistication of analysis any existing system'. (*Journal for the Study of Consciousness*). This might appear to be a sweeping statement for a scientist to make, though anyone trained in astrology and psychology will readily understand and accept such a view.

By now, those of you who have always associated astrology with fortune-telling and reading the future may be wondering how this actually fits into the scheme of things, especially since we have only been dealing so far with astrology and personality.

The Nature of Time

Fortune-telling, clairvoyance and second sight were of great interest to Jung in his later years. He believed that scientific investigation into these kind of phenomena could tell us a great deal more about the workings of the mind, and after exhaustive researches he was able to formulate his own theories as to the principles involved. In order to convey to you the general idea of what second sight or predicting the future may entail, I am going to simplify the complexity of abstract philosophy and laws of science that Jung, of course, utilized to the full, and present what I hope is a reasonably clear picture with a minimum of technical or obscure words.

Before we procede, however, I should like you to check on your own particular thoughts about time.

If you have ever wondered about crystal-gazing or any other means for 'looking' into the future, you must have given some consideration to time—what it is, and if it exists. If your immediate reaction to this is that it exists, then we need to pause and reflect for a moment. Time has become a tangible asset in society. But time, clearly, is man-made. This is evident enough, but we take it so much for granted we sometimes forget that it is actually the orderly cycles of nature and the universe that establish a *sense* of time. Stop the earth from turning and there would be no sunrise, noon, sunset, or lunar month.

Man's conception of day, night, month and year would never have evolved but for the fact that our little world revolves constantly upon its axis in the void of infinite space. The apparent movement of the heavenly bodies marks a regular pattern, or duration, as from one sunrise to the next. Thus, our view of time is based upon movement. You can look at it another way—a plant bursts into life, not because the time is right, only because particular conditions trigger the seed into activity. And from its sprouting, through its flowering, fruiting, until the withering away, it is movement, energy, the life-force that has marked a period, or duration of an event, from a beginning to an end. This is so evident, so fundamental to our existence, that it is not surprising if we tend to lose sight of it; but this kind of view will help to grasp what follows. Incidentally, it does illustrate very well just how significant is the constant universal rhythm, even though we are not always aware of it.

Why is it that so many people dream of events that later on turn out to have happened, or do happen, in reality? It is such a widely shared and frequent experience that most readers will have little difficulty in accepting this. Jung's 'archetypes' and 'collective unconscious', referred to previously, will provide us with the stepping-stones into the stream of time-sense. It is in the deeper levels of the unconscious mind that the curious phenomenom of visioning (second sight) begins to take shape.

The general run of nightly dreams contains the imagery and impressions that mainly arise from the 'personal unconscious', but sometimes a dream seems to take on much more significance, and we wake up wondering what it meant. This response is natural, for, more often than not, the deeper unconscious is sending a message —by means of the archetypal-images—to consciousness, because there is probably a need to adjust the balance in our lives in some way. But these images are of a primal nature, shared by all, in every era of civilization—echoes of our evolution and struggle. They are the archetypes of birth and dying, of nature and human beings, and of the universe, and they await within the collective unconscious, formless, but ever ready to become symbols of dream material— messages that preserve the natural balance of self and society.

It is as if we all have a basic circuit of common experience, though we sometimes fail to recognize the fact. It can be triggered into action when we deviate from our natural course, or when external forces happen to correspond with particular archetypes. Jung actually anticipated the First and Second World Wars in the process of analyzing the dreams of many patients. It is as though there is a common emotional denominator at the collective unconscious level, waiting to externalize. In this respect, it is well to remember that although we may be swayed by world events, let us say, if we have a true inner harmony we are unlikely to respond to outer disharmony. And conversely, when there is inward disquiet it requires a shift of attention and an alteration in perspective if we are not to be continually responding to every eddy in external conditions.

It could be reasoned that Jung was enabled to forecast events by his knowledge of dream symbols, and indeed he wrote and spoke extensively about his conclusions and fears, although very few people took him seriously at the time. What this shows, however, is that there is a capacity within the human mind to respond to stored impressions when there is an appropriate external stimulus, even if we are not immediately aware of what the stimulus might be. It is quite possible that this ability is linked to the age-old instinct for self-preservation and the maintenance of the species. Jung built up his picture of an oncoming threat through the unconscious material of others—at second hand, as it were—but it could be said, therefore, that some individuals, those with a clairvoyant gift, have an open-line to the collective unconscious. We say that they are able to 'see' things. Crystal-gazers actually 'see' images in their crystal-balls, though these are recognized as projections from the unconscious, and in fact are usually in the form of symbols that have to be interpreted. In other words, the seer is observing dream material while apparently awake, or partially awake, i.e., in a trance-like state. This material, as you will have guessed, is comprised of the archetypes, and in some respects is similar to the symbolism of tarot cards, whose symbols are very definitely of an archetypal nature, Playing cards, too, are used for fortune-telling, although their symbolism is numerical. We shall be looking at 'number' archetypes later on.

Synchronicity

It seems as though, therefore, there is a natural faculty of the mind to 'tune-in' to external influences, and that it is more likely to respond to those influences which are on the same 'wave-length'. And, just like a radio or television receiver, the incoming impressions or impulses have to be altered into a visual form before they can be recognized, and the form or imagery has to be brought into clear focus—by the intellect—before the true meaning becomes apparent.

All the phenomena of second sight, looking into the future, etc., Jung termed 'synchronicity', which in general parlance could be called meaningful coincidence. He derived his views from lengthy investigation and research into mythology and Eastern philosophy, though always maintaining a strictly scientific approach. Let me see if I can convey to you something of his conception of how our minds work and respond to the sense of time, or rather, the spanning of time.

Everything that occurs has a cause. We accept that things

happen because something in the past caused them to happen. It can also be observed that circumstances come about because of the plan or purpose they serve. If we put these two views together we are presented with a consideration that goes something like this: Because it is in the very nature of the personality (the mind) to gather from the past in order to pave a way to the future, while relating and responding to the present, it is possible that the cause (past), the purpose (present), and the objective (future), may be visualized as a whole. It is as though, because of the faculty to extend consciousness back and forth along a sequence of events, an awareness of time is possible. Even at the biological level there are on-going cycles of response that help maintain the progressive rhythms of life and nature. I say 'progressive' because once a thing commences it goes on until its duration is completed. In a way, there is a natural bias towards forward viewing that arises out of the regular, universal motions, as well as from the instinctive urge to survive.

The ability to view sequences or circumstances as a whole is not a thing that some people find easy to understand, although, as Jung explained, the Eastern mind is completely in tune with this principle. For example, we might hear of a multiple pile-up on the motor-way, and our immediate thoughts might be, 'Why do they drive like that? I wonder what the road conditions were like? Wasn't the traffic control efficient enough?' But the Eastern mind would be asking, 'What does this event mean? What was significant about the time it occured?' We tend to observe facts separately, while the Eastern mind more readily accepts a group of facts as a conglomerate, and looks for a meaning in the whole.

The I Ching

The Chinese doctrine of Tao, 'The Way', exemplifies the Eastern philosophy and approach to life. This is also demonstrated in the ancient Chinese method of divination known as the I Ching. When Jung first spoke of such things in the thirties, very few people in the West appreciated what he was talking about. Nowadays, the I Ching is a highly popular system of fortune-telling. It relies upon an apparently random selection of sticks, placed in piles to produce six numbers, making a hexagram. It is the symbolism of the numbers that form the basis of the reading or prediction.

I used the word 'apparently' because is it altogether chance that sticks, dice, cards or coins fall the way they do when we throw for the purpose of revealing what is hidden from consciousness? As Jung suggested, and as psychologists are beginning to realize, there is more going on within the deeper layers of the unconscious than was at one time believed, and it is not beyond reason to suppose that minute, muscle reflexes could be affected by the subconscious impulses from activated archetypes.

Many years ago, a friend, who happened to be a clairvoyant, came to me for a forecast analysis. Because she had sometimes told me things about my own life that she could not possibly have known by ordinary means, I was curious to know why she did not apply her obvious gift for second sight to her own life. She explained that it would be considered 'bad luck' to tell one's own fortune.

Psychology explains why this is so. Have you noticed that when you are really enjoying yourself, either at work or play, you are so completely absorbed in the present that there is no inclination to concern yourself about the past or the future? When there is stress and worry, however, we are continually asking ourselves what went wrong, and how will things turn out. My friend, understandably, had no wish to use her ability for extending awareness in her own life because of the additional burden that it would entail. She required, at that time, a detached and constructive view of her problems.

As an astrologer I can understand this. Although I do not have any special gift, it is perfectly possible to scan time by projecting the planetary patterns to any period with the aid of the astronomical references, and making an assessment of the likely psychological and emotional experiences for any period. From this, the likely type of conditions or circumstances can be inferred, though no definite event can be 'predicted'. This is why no serious astrologer ever claims to predict, only to forecast trends. Anyway, as the quickest way to learn how a chart works is to use one's own, it is possible to see the developments in one's own life all too clearly. This sort of knowledge, therefore, imposes a burden of responsibility that requires an integrated and philosophical outlook on life. For this reason, students of astrology who feel they do not want to 'know the worst about themselves' can always leave their own chart, and get on with the study of others.

There is a moral behind all this, of course, and it is that we should get on with what we enjoy doing best, now, in the present, rather than be overly concerned for the morrow.

Logic and Intuition

However, to return to the way we look at time, or things in general, and the difference between the two types of mind which Jung observed as 'Eastern' and 'Western'. There is, in fact, a more up-to-date attempt at describing such tendencies. A few years ago, Dr Edward de Bono wrote a very popular book, *Lateral Thinking,* in which he presented views that were similar to Jung's in this respect. There is, he suggests, the formal, logical way of thinking, in which facts are taken in a set order, in the process of reaching a conclusion. This, he terms 'vertical' thinking. But when the mind extends around the subject and arrives at a conclusion, almost as though by intuition, this he calls 'lateral' thinking. He evolved exercises for encouraging the mind in lateral thinking, because it is this type of mental ability that most effectively solves difficult problems, and his work is much valued in industry and commerce.

Astrologically, these two differing ways of looking at things are very nicely represented by the pair of opposite signs, Virgo-Pisces. The Virgo type is often notorious for an insistence upon attention to the orderly arrangement of fact and detail, while the Piscean swims happily in a sea of perceptive intuitivity, carefully avoiding the rocks of hard fact. Interestingly enough, it takes a combination of the opposites to lift an individual above the mean average of ability in any sphere of life.

By chance, I have had two accountants among my clients, both successful in establishing their own firms. One is a Piscean (sun) with strong Virgoan undertones, and the other a Virgo, with marked Piscean qualities. Everyone knows that an accountant must be good at figures, but it requires that extra dimension to be able to read a page of figures and see the picture as a whole. The most successful business men, we read, are not only practical, but able to rely upon their 'hunches' to a remarkable degree.

This suggests, does it not, that there is a very real advantage in trying to discover our full potentials, and not just stumbling along on a 'wing and a prayer'. The personality is rather like a car engine. If it is not firing on all cylinders its performance is halting and ragged. For example, stress for a markedly Virgoan type could easily arise from continually worrying about matters of detail, over-conscientiousness, and wondering why others cannot understand or sympathize (Piscean counterbalance) with them. Anxiety, for an out-and-out Piscean could be caused or exacerbated by the desire to escape from the hard facts (Virgoan counterbalance) and to wallow in a sea of confusion or self-pity. The same reasoning can be applied to each pair of opposites.

Psychologically, and here I am referring to Jung's more formal classification of function types, these opposites have their parallel with sensation (Virgo) and intuition (Pisces), although a bias towards any one function does not rely, astrologically, upon the sun signs alone, but also to various planetary couplings, as we shall discover in the next chapter.

In this chapter we have dealt with some quite complex and abstract ideas, mainly from a psychological standpoint. Before concluding, I should like to indicate an interesting feature that became apparent to me when I was trying to evolve the deeper psychological interpretations of the sun signs.

By chance, it was found that the list of thirty-six personality tendencies could be sub-divided into four categories, and that these appeared to correspond very closely with the four functions: thinking, feeling, sensation, intuition. For this reason, the wording of each interpretation is designed to convey an indication of which function or functions are liable to be most vulnerable, and therefore which conditions might prove to be stress-making ones. Again, there are no hard-and-fast indications to be adhered to, but general pointers which may be seen as useful guidelines.

To clarify the list references regarding the functions, we might visualize the possibility of stress arising from:

1. Difficulties in relationships (Feeling).
2. Problems in the desire to understand and be understood (Thinking).
3. Problems which challenge the sense of security, or reality (Sensation).
4. Obstacles to the expression of independence or personal freedom (Intuition).

It will be clear that not every personality description can be limited to a single function, and an attempt has been made to suggest the various combinations that appear to be present. For example, the first interpretation in the list, 1-10 January, shows that we have a mixture of sensation and feeling as the probable dominant functions. It would therefore be an advantage to encourage the opposites of thinking and intuition, if either appear to be neglected.

On the other hand, in the second interpretation, 11-20 January (still a sun Capricorn, you will note), the traits of the sensation type remain, but now thinking is to the fore; and here we might imagine, for example, a patient, industrious, possibly ambitious person whose main interests are concerned with achieving material security. If, in fact, the bias is too much that way, then the anxieties will be due to a lack of feeling-relating, and/or intuitivity, in some way or other.

Obviously, it is impossible to give neat little answers to every likely stress problem, because of the infinite variety of human experience and response, though I hope I have shown that astrology can be a useful adjunct to the better understanding of personality.

I have started from the platform of psychology because most people can understand emotions, feelings and behaviour, even in a general way, though very few people have any real knowledge of astrology or its terminology, except in the vaguest way. But having prepared the ground in this chapter, it should be possible for you to now follow general astrological principles, as outlined in the next chapter.

5. THE ASTROLOGY
OF PSYCHOLOGY

Is one sun sign more prone to stress than another?

This is a question that the astrologer is often asked. Although it is a generalization to say that Pisces or Cancer, for instance, are more sensitive than Taurus or Capricorn, the evidence of the Mayo-Eysenck paper alone would be sufficient to support the idea that there is a variability of response that appears to synchronize with the movement of the sun in its annual cycle around the ecliptic. In the calculation of the individual chart, even the movement of sun, moon and planets, minute by minute, is of utmost importance.

The various shades of stress, whether experienced as nervous tension, anxiety or depression, are clearly defined by the intricate planetary patterns present at the moment of birth. Some insight into the basic principles involved in astrological analysis may be useful here.

Astrological Opposites

I have already made reference to the law of opposites, and this will serve as a useful platform to work from. This law operates most noticeably in the wheel of the zodiac (ecliptic) itself. Each sign is compensated and polarized through its opposite, and, likewise, each sub-division has its compliment. We could even go further and observe each degree and its opposite, in the three hundred and sixty degrees of the ecliptic. The list comprises thirty-six interpretations, and this is because I sub-divided each of the signs into three, following an ancient practice in Hindu astrology.

When sections of a sign are examined individually a curious phenomenon becomes apparent. The sun's expression—in the astrological sense—does not remain constant and of the nature of the sign throughout its length, but alters slightly as it passes through each ten degrees—a sign being thirty degrees in length. I think that most readers will know that each sign has its 'ruling planet'. For example, Mars is the ruler of Aries, Venus the ruler of Libra, Sun rules Leo, and so on. However, the quality of a ruling planet appears to be most dominant in the first section of its sign. Thereafter, other planets' natures modify each section, and the way in which this comes about is based upon the formal sequence of the elements.

With the nature of three planets subtly altering each sign, it means that we can follow the modifications to the sun's expression in each sign more closely, and also observe the interplay between each sub-section and its opposite. It is as though each sign has three planetary pairs, and certainly, in practice, it is of additional help in the interpretation of the sun, or any other body, to take into consideration the underlying influence that a particular section of the sign may have.

The thirty-six pairs are made up of the natures of the ten bodies, Sun, Moon, Mercury, Venus, Mars, etc. For example, Mars-Venus, Moon-Saturn, Mercury-Jupiter and so on. From these it is possible to isolate all the constituent parts of our four functions: thinking-feeling, sensation-intuition. But this is not surprising since they derive from the symbolism of the four Elements in the first place.

The Elements

The elements, fire, earth, air and water, have been observed in symbolic form by philosophers, healers, astrologers, and others for at least two and half thousand years. The ancients—by which I mean those of our earliest forebears who were already laying down the foundations of science as we know it today—believed that all things were created from the four elements, and therefore, it was only natural to them to explain human physiology and behaviour in the light of their then limited knowledge. They reasoned that a dominance of an element in an individual would be reflected in the personality. In fact, Jung's four function types have their origins in the four 'humours' of antiquity: choleric (fire), phlegmatic (earth), sanguine (air), and melancholic (water). The elements are of a primal nature, their symbolism bound up in mythology, and were an integral part of the alchemy of the Middle Ages. As Jung so succinctly put it, 'Our conscious scientific mind started in the matrix of the unconscious mind.'

The psychological qualities generally associated with the elements, in astrology, are: Fire = active, impulsive; Earth = stable, practical; Air = intellectual, communicative; Water = sensitive, emotional. Each sign is allocated an element in the traditional order: Aries-Fire, Taurus-Earth, Gemini-Air, Cancer-Water, Leo-Fire, Virgo-Earth, and so on. A fact that is so simple that it is often overlooked is the marvellous way in which the order of the elements—always adhered to—so aptly reveals the logical progression of creation and evolution as it is instinctively felt within the collective unconscious of mankind. The fact that it is in perfect accord with modern scientific thought is quite evident. Scientists tell us that the universe was a spinning, fiery mass (Fire), from which parts—our earth and the planets—flew off, and in cooling to a solid (Earth), gave off gases (Air), that eventually precipitated to form the oceans (Water).

It is even possible to pursue the sequence and the symbolism of creation further. In the vastness of time and human evolution, life began to develop (out of the oceans, so we are told) and a consciousness of the environment became imprinted upon the minds of our earliest, sentient ancestors—a race-memory that was eventually to be recorded and handed down throughout the ages. In Genesis, for example, there is an allusion to this in the words: 'And the Spirit of God moved upon the face of the waters. And God said, Let there be light, and there was light.' Even this biblical symbolism picks up the sequence, since after the first of the water signs, the second fire sign, Leo—'ruled' by the sun, giver of light—follows on.

The symbolism of the elements, and indeed of each heavenly body that comprises our tiny universe, is so profound, so fundamental to the structures of civilization, and so intricately woven into the fabric of each and every personality, that it is like a revelation of the Divine Order just to contemplate this symbolism. In the light of such understanding, one experiences a profound joy.

There is no real secret in this, any more than there is in the attainment of tranquillity and contentment in the midst of life's tensions. A thing is only mysterious when it is not properly understood at the conscious level. Symbols, just like letters, words, sentences and numbers, give meaning to the abstracts of the unconscious mind, and are the keys to a realization of the perfect peace of soul that is always with us, even though, in the chaos of living, we sometimes lose sight of the fact.

In most astrological books attempts are usually made to align the four functions with the elements rather than with the sectional polarizations, which I have termed planetary pairs. The only exception I have come across is Dane Rudhyar's excellent work, *An Astrological Study of Psychological Complexes and Emotional Problems,* first published in 1966. In this, he lists four 'major urges or drives' as being the main root cause for stress and anxiety, and examines several combinations of planets that are similar to the ones I have indicated: the urge to be a particular being (Moon-Saturn), the urge to preserve the characteristic form of that being (Jupiter-Mercury), the reproductive urge (Mars-Venus), and the desire to transform (Uranus-Neptune). All but the last can be found in the pairs of opposites, but of course, he is looking at these from the point of view of their disposition and angular relationship within the birth chart.

Let us look at the third item, the urge to reproduce. The symbols for Mars ♂ and Venus ♀ are universally recognized as representing male and female. Mars is synonymous with heat and energy and Venus with love and affection. Put the two together and what do we have? Passion, of course! Thus, if we were to examine the birth chart of somebody with a sexual problem, this is the pair that would come under special consideration. In the psychological context they are very much of the nature of the feeling function. When they occur as an underlying modification of a sign's sub-division, I have interpreted them as having reference to relationships, e.g., as in 10-19 February, 14-23 August.

The fact that the observation of polar opposites aids interpretation, even when broad-based as in sun sign sections, will be confirmed by the reasonably high level of validity to be found in the list interpretations. In an individual chart, with hundreds of factors to be evaluated, it is of great help to be able to select the relevant pair for special attention. Of course, in a birth chart more than two planets may combine in angular relationship, and these will invariably constitute a complex that will be an obvious feature of the personality. In this, you can readily appreciate how it is that the astrologer, even without formal training in psychoanalysis, has an enormous advantage over any psychologist when it comes to personality assessment.

Using Astrological Knowledge

In the last chapter I outlined what might be termed the psychology of fortune-telling, and indicated the two ways of viewing time and circumstances. The Eastern, intuitive type of mind being, perhaps, better able to comprehend an event as a whole, as though encompassing a span of time. This is an area of much contention, one doctrine proclaiming that there is no such thing as time, only 'Now', and another actively questioning this and presenting evidence to support the claim that it does exist. One view relies heavily upon the principle that everything has a beginning (causality), and the other that everything develops because of the purpose that is served (teleology).

In general terms, we might see such differences existing between, let us say, the spiritual views of a church man, and the questioning of a materialistic scientist, who demands proof that there is a God. These differing viewpoints illustrate how poles apart we can be in our outlook, and serve to show why you may or may not find it easy to accept astrological principles. Fortunately, however, the advantage of astrology as a forecasting system is that, unlike most methods for 'telling the future', it does not require any special type of mind, because all the assumptions are based upon readily available factors, i.e., the astronomical tables. By observing the planetary movements for any given period (and it is as easy to check backwards in time as it is to go forwards), it is possible to *infer* the sort of psychological colouring that may develop, and to put that knowledge to good use. Here is an instance of this.

Some years ago, a clinician asked me to do a chart projection for a highly-strung patient who had been going through a critical phase. An assessment of all the planetary complexes for the year ahead revealed when the emotional peaks might occur, and so the therapist was prepared in advance, and could give some extra attention to the patient just when it was needed. It has always seemed to me that a closer cooperation between astrologers and psychologists could eventually produce very valuable guidelines for the practical application of astrological techniques. There is nothing mysterious about astrological forecasting, other than the mystique created by misconception. No serious astrologer ever claims to 'predict' the future, since this implies an ability to describe an actual event. As you can see, we are dealing with the variables of human response as they appear to correlate with planetary movements.

Of course, any suggestion that human behaviour seems to be modified by planetary movements draws forth the inevitable question, 'Are we really influenced by the stars?' Well, we are certainly influenced by many things. In some people, items of diet, like flour, coffee, and sugar, cause restlessness, anxiety and even panic states. Cut down the amount of oxygen in the air we breath by a fraction, and we become lethargic; increase our normal living temperature and irritability is soon apparent. In the years before strong tranquillizers, mental nurses feared the days around the time of the full moon, because they knew that there would be an increase of violence on the wards. Nowadays, it is often an increase in emergency admissions that they have to contend with. Some police departments in America have observed from their records that there are usually more road accidents around the time of the full moon. Years ago, in an article on astrology, I read that graphs for sun spot and stock-market activity followed the same pattern. I was reminded of this at the beginning of 1980, when the selling and buying of gold reached an all-time high. Everyone seemed to get the gold fever. Being curious, I asked an astronomer friend what the sun spot reading was. You can guess his reply—very high indeed!

Applications of Astrological Insights

We are long past the stage of asking if astrology really works. Of course it does. What is required now is a more positive approach to the subject on the part of the scientific body. Not that they all behave in an ostrich-like manner, of course. As we have seen, Jung was the first to acknowledge its contribution to scientific under-standing. Professor Eysenck, in his cooperation with Jeff Mayo, has made a valuable contribution. At the Institute of Psychiatry's astrological conference, papers were presented on such subjects as astrology's relationship to neuro-endocrinological development, effects on the pineal gland, lunar rhythms and human activity, neuroticism, and so on. Over the years, I have been most fortunate in the encouragement and time afforded me by men who are authorities in the fields of psychology and psychiatry. For instance, one consultant, for whom I had done an astro-analysis for a patient, wrote to me a kind letter observing that if the problem of therapy could be tackled with astrological knowledge, the insight of the therapist would be greatly aided.

Clearly, busy hospital consultants do not have a great deal of time to spend on research matters, and there is little likelihood of hospital authorities putting astrologers on the pay-role! But the employment of astrological techniques could eventually prove to have some real advantages in cost and time-effectiveness.

In the present state of affairs, anyone seeking relief for a neurosis or phobia (fear) has to make do with drugs, or some form of group therapy—popular, not because it is always appropriate for the individual, but because it is less time consuming to deal with a number of patients at one go. But, psychoanalysis, considered to be of great value in the treatment of anxiety neuroses, has to take a back seat, because it is so time consuming. Yet it is not an exaggeration to suggest that, in many cases, access to astro-analysis would enable a busy therapist to more rapidly obtain a deeper insight into a case, thus reducing the number of sessions required.

Marriage Problems

Before closing this chapter, there is one area of our lives which, unhappily, seems to have suffered an increase of stress and disruption in the past decade, and in which astrological techniques can provide some help—marriage. We say that the increase of separations is to due to modern trends, or the 'permissive society'; yet we seem to be incapable of doing anything about it. The emotional pressures that society has burdened our young people with is considerable, but it is as though we are all caught up in the web of the collective atmosphere. Objections to material put out by the media receive the inevitable answer that it is what the public wants, or that, 'as a work of art, it is only reflecting life'. There is an element of truth in this, whether we like it or not.

Previously, we saw how Jung noticed common emotional factors acting within the deep levels of the collective unconscious of many of his patients while in the process of analyzing their dreams, and how from this he was able to draw the impression of the threat of conflict before both the 1914 and 1939 World Wars. Little notice was taken of his forecasts, even after the Second World War; so when it is suggested that astrologers, especially those dealing with mundane or political astrology, are continually aware of the underlying emotional currents of society, the assertion is difficult to accept by some people. This is not to say that astrologers can predict war or anything else with any more certainty than anyone else, but that they do have a finger on the cosmic pulse, and major tendencies can be and are assessed. Let us take a broad view of the past twenty years, as an example.

In the early sixties there was a very noticeable increase of disruptive behaviour in the youth of many countries. In particular, we heard a great deal about student revolts, sit-ins, etc. There was something of a running battle between students and authority for the best part of this decade, and no one could have missed the continual stream of incidents from college campus and university that was reported by the media. Now, between the end of 1961 and 1968, Uranus moved through the sign of Virgo. The symbolism here is so explicit that there should be no difficulty in understanding it. Uranus stands for, self-will, change, and reformistic tendencies. Virgo, the sign of the virgin, symbolizes the teenage phase of development, as well as being related to knowledge and learning.

During the latter part of the sixties and into the early seventies, not only did we see increasing tension between the sexes—manifesting in movements (Uranian factor) like 'Women's Lib'—but also a growing intransigence between one country and another. By this time, Uranus had moved from Virgo into Libra, the sign of relatedness and partnerships. It was followed, in 1971, by Pluto, a planet which intensifies emotional response, and sometimes marks crises points, throwing to light that which has been festering below the surface.

By the mid-seventies, with Pluto still in Libra and Uranus now into Scorpio, the sign of deep emotions and sensuality, we saw a period in which sexual revelations of a kind that were hitherto thought unmentionable were now openly discussed on television. (The essence of the Uranian factor is 'rhythmic processes', which link it directly to waves, light, radio, etc.) Good ladies spoke about their bladder operations, we were treated to the sight of births for the first time, normal and caesarian, in full colour, and homosexuals not only basked in the light of the television arcs, but demanded recognition and a new deal.

Whether or not you accept that patterns of behaviour in society can be deduced from the transits of planets, the fact remains that there has been a climate of change in our attitude to sex and relationships. Changes often bring a period of upset and stress in their wakes. This we have to accept, in the light of greater understanding and compassion that accompanies any change. But, would it have been helpful to have prior knowledge of change, just supposing that astrological observations were available in advance. The answer is surely obvious.

However, to move from the general to the particular, astrology does have a very real and valuable function in the area of marriage counselling. A fair proportion of any astrological practice is taken up with requests for compatibility assessments. This entails comparing the chart of one partner with the other, and as it is an uncomplex and graphic way of revealing every psychological facet between two individuals, it enables the astrologer to perceive the strengths and weaknesses of any liaison in a way that would be the envy of marriage guidance counsellors. In this, I am not suggesting that astrologers do a better job, but that the employment of astrological techniques could effectively assist the counsellor to achieve deeper insights into a case far more quickly than is possible by the usual methods of lengthy investigation and questioning.

There is a common belief, among followers of popular astrology, that various of the sun signs 'go together', and within the obvious limitations of generalization, this is so. Earlier on, we discussed the elements and how they were allocated to the signs. It seems reasonable to suppose that people sharing the qualities of a particular element are more likely to be in accord. Therefore, as a broad, rule-of-thumb, some guidance can be obtained through a knowledge of individuals' sun signs. The elements are distributed like this:

Fire: Aries, Leo, Saggittarius.
Earth: Taurus, Virgo, Capricorn.
Air: Gemini, Libra, Aquarius.
Water: Cancer, Scorpio, Pisces.

Obviously, the consulting astrologer observes the many links between charts, and any deductions that may be made are done in the light of all considerations possible; but a sensible reasoning about any two signs and their elements will often come surprisingly close to the truth. People sharing the same sign usually get along well, though may experience some irritations, just because they are so similar. There is usually plenty of emotional steam when a Fire and Water type get together, and just as fire can either evaporate water, or be damped down by it, so too can it burn brighter in the presence of oxygen (Air), and there is likely to be plenty of spirited discussion when Fire and Air get together.

Sometimes, Water and Earth signs combine well, in just the same way as the ocean is held by the land. Watery Pisces may find the practicality of a Virgo reassuring, or the depths of a Scorpio may find security in the material stability of Taurus. These are the sort of allegories that anyone can reason out for themselves, for any combination of signs that may happen to be of interest.

Of course, the astrologer has just the same problems in advising as does the marriage guidance counsellor. Sometimes an individual asks for a compatibility analysis, not entirely because they wish to achieve a better understanding of themselves and their partner, but because they want to use the astrological report as a reason for separation. As in all areas of life, the utilization of astrology must be seen as an aid to greater understanding, not as a tool for the manipulation of others.

6. THE ASTROLOGICAL JIGSAW

In an earlier chapter I referred to the correlation between high levels of sun spot activity and extremes on the world's stock-markets, reflecting, as it does, variations in the pattern of human behaviour. This is easier to understand when it is realized that sun spot activity affects the earth's electromagnetic field, and it is certain that biological structures, as well as human responses, are subtly modified by disturbances in the earth's magnetic field.

Many people suffer from acute anxiety during electric storms. Scientists now use electromagnetic microwaves to alter enzyme activity in the body in order to mend slow healing fractures. The clotting time of blood varies with the monthly lunar cycle, presumably for the same reason—i.e., that it creates a continual flux in the electromagnetic field. Even metallic salts react in a specific and demonstrable way, in synchronization with the movement of planets. This has been observed in clear-cut experiments, carried out under controlled laboratory conditions, and is based upon the traditional idea that each planet has its own metal. e.g., iron accords with Mars, lead with Saturn, etc.

There are numerous items like these, scientific jigsaw pieces that fit effectively into the astrological picture, and are readily found in specialist journals and the world's astrological literature. However, I would like to touch upon another sort of jigsaw; one that reveals an intriguing picture of the levels of consciousness.

At the beginning of this book I promised an explanation of how it became possible for me to derive a more detailed, psychological interpretation from the sun signs. The astrological basis is an ancient and well-known one, being the division of the ecliptic into thirty-six instead of twelve sections. As we have seen already, this does provide a framework from which a little more information per sign can be obtained, but it does not in any way clarify interpretation or make it more meaningful. Some development is possible by observing the interplay of opposites, but that is about as far as one would normally go. The casually interested person generally avoids exploration into fundamental principles, and the serious astrologer usually wants to deal with the intriguing complexities of a fully calculated birth chart. So it was that when I wanted to construct a more meaningful list of interpretations for a wider public I had to search around for alternative methods for extracting and handling the symbolism of the zodiac.

The Insights of Numerology

Astrology is very much tied up with numerology, and this seemed to me to be a promising line of approach, especially as Jung had considered 'number' of much importance to the understanding of the archetypal images of the unconscious mind. Number, in this sense, refers to the qualitative and not the quantitative value we normally associate with the numerical symbols.

Numerology, as the study of the qualitative value of numbers, has long a popular method of fortune telling, but only in comparatively recent times have scientists come to realize that the mind actually works on numerical principles, and that number is at the very foundation of our thought processes. It is even possible to trace the links back to the biological level. Marie-Louise von Franz, in her erudite work, *Number and Time,* puts it this way: 'When energy manifests itself in either psychic or physical dimensions, it is always ''numerically'' structured, e.g., as ''waves'' or as (psychic) rhythm.' She also points out that D.N.A., the molecular structure of life, is composed of four bases from which are derived sixty-four different triplets. These form a genetic code which is conveyed to the cells. What is fascinating is that, numerically, reflections of these basic structures of the living organism can be found in thought processes. This is particularly evident in the I Ching, an oracle providing a simple method for symbolizing the contents of the unconscious, which is based upon sixty-four, three line structures.

References to the figures two, three and four come up time and again in religion, legend and myth, e.g., the Trinity, the three bears, three wishes, four witches, etc. Two is fundamental to relationships, the hero and heroine, mother and father, and so on. These numbers are also integral to the formal structure of the horoscopic circle.

Numerical Symbolism in the Horoscope

When a chart is first drawn, the horizon line is placed, thus dividing the circle into upper and lower sections, which are equivalent, in actuality, to south and north, and symbolically to the public and private aspects of life, or, conscious and unconscious, day and night, light and dark, and so on. At this rudimentary stage the chart is similar to the Ying-Yang symbol of Chinese philosophy, in which the circle contains a light and a dark half, analogous (equal) to the male and female principles, interlocked, and forever endeavouring to achieve unity and balance.

When two is viewed from the psychological standpoint it is said to represent the 'dualistic structure of threshold phenomena'. This is explained by dream analysis, when a person dreams of a pair of anything, and in particular when one dreams of one's double. This usually signals that further dream material may be forthcoming from the deeper layers of the unconscious, and such material is often most valuable in providing helpful information which can help to restore the balance between the conscious and unconscious life of the personality.

When the horizon line is cut by a vertical line, marking the zenith and nadir, a cross is formed, thus creating four sub-sections (Jung found the symbol of the cross within the circle to be a highly significant figure, featuring in myth and the earliest religious ornamentation). Four is the first square number, and in numer-ological interpretation represents the traits of self-will and determination. The psychological definition suggests that it implies the psychic centre, or 'closed structure of human consciousness'. In its geometric, graphic form within the circle of the ecliptic (horoscope), it constitutes a point of actualization—precipitating emotional energy into event.

The four sectors of the circle are further divided into three, thus making the twelve houses of the horoscope. Three, the first triangular number, symbolizes the dynamic energy flow of consciousness into actualization. In numerological terms, three may be said to have the character of enthusiasm and harmonious expression, with the qualities of expansiveness and sociability.

It is not my intention to give you a detailed account of numerology, but to just convey how number can be seen rather like a universal matrix from which psychological structures may come into being, and how number forms an integral framework within the zodiacal circle. Obviously the 360 degrees of the ecliptic are not confined to astrology but have been a framework of reference for astronomers and navigators from the earliest times. Even students of astrology sometimes overlook the fact that astrology, as a subject for exploring the world of the mind, has exactly the same numerical framework by which man finds his way about the physical world and universe.

The first thing I did when I came to consider the possible advantage of thirty-six rather than twelve divisions was to assess the number values of each. In numerology the practice is to reduce double figures to one digit by addition. Hence, twelve becomes three $(1 + 2)$, and thirty-six becomes nine $(3 + 6)$. In so far as the individual birth chart with its twelve houses is representative of the individual personality and potential in total it accords well with the 'three' principle. On the other hand, nine is found at the end of the decimal sequence, symbolizing the final product. In Indian astrology, a chart formulated on base nine is said to represent the fruits of one's endeavours. Viewed in this light I felt that our thirty-six sign division stood a better chance of conveying the working-out of sun signs potentialities and revealing something of the expression or experience of the mature personality.

Harmonics

The consideration of number brought me to the subject of harmonics in astrology, and as this is something that I don't think the general reader will be familiar with, let me apologize, and suggest that you will lose little if you simply skip the following section.

By viewing the decanates as a thirty-sixth harmonic it becomes possible to formulate mid-point structures quite readily between the planetary principles of each sub-section. For example, the structure for the third decanate of Gemini can be expressed like this: ♊ ♅ ⚥/♇ . Here we can readily see the intensification of the thinking function that could be interpreted as 'fanatical pursuit of one's plans. Nervous breakdown through overtaxing one's own strength', to quote from Ebertin's *The Combination of Stellar Influences.*

The sun is centred in the third decanate of Gemini around 17 June, when it is close to the 25th degree of the sign, and at a position indicated by Carter in *An Encyclopaedia of Psychological Astrology* as increasing the likelihood of 'neurasthenia' and hyper-sensitivity. Naturally, the same structure is highlighted again when the Sun moves through the 25th degree of Sagittarius, also designated a 'sensitive' area.

Students familiar with harmonics and mid-points will find that an examination of the potentiality for any sector, in terms of these combined structures, will be found to be extremely helpful and revealing. In my interpretations I have, of course, made use of Carter's list of degree areas, which have some, if limited, statistical verification, but it is most interesting to observe that the decanate —harmonic—mid-point structures and the degree areas do, for the most part, reinforce and confirm each other.

Having got to a stage when I was satisfied that it was possible to extract as much as could be reasonably expected from every sector of the ecliptic, I was still left with the problem of adequate inter-pretation. Obscurity and ambiguity are the bugbears of astrological jargon. There is no excuse for either of these in individual chart analysis, but I did want to make some attempt, at least, in reducing generalization during the process of constructing the interpre-tations. Like most astrologers, I am familiar with the technical language of Jungian, analytical psychology, but it did not seem appropriate for my purpose, so I had to search for alternatives.

Astrology and Colour

Happily, the problem was solved quite easily while I was perusing the literature of another area of symbolism and human response—colour. Just as number is analogous to energy patterns, which have their counterpart in the archetypes of the unconscious, so too does colour have its particular properties of vibration which are synonymous with mood. Fortunately, too, a great deal of reliable statistical work has been carried out in the field of colour and human behaviour—in particular, the work of Dr M. Luscher, who evolved a simple but highly effective psychological test using eight colour cards.

There are long-established links between astrology and colour, each sign having its own colour. For example, red is considered the colour of Aries, gold that of Leo, electric blue that of Aquarius, etc. When one reads the psychological attributes applied to a colour it is easy to see the similarity with its astrological equivalent. For instance, Jeff Mayo, in his *Teach Yourself Astrology* gives Geminian traits as: '. . . variability and spontaneity. Is adaptable, communicative, versatile. Incessantly on the go, restless, inquisitive . . .', and so on. Very much the same can be found in the earlier textbooks, but the interesting thing is that a Geminian colour is yellow, and Dr Luscher's interpretation of bright yellow lists the following interpretation of bright yellow lists the following psychological qualities: 'Spontaneity, ex-centric (i.e., interested in people and things), active, projective, heteronomous (draws stimulus from the environment), aspiring and investigatory'.

As the colours in Dr Luscher's test do have a correlation with the four functions, and as combinations of colours form personality traits or complexes in the same way as the structures that I had evolved, I discovered that not only was it possible to confirm one's own ideas about the meaning of any combination of symbols (signs and planetary principles), but that the descriptive language of functional (colour) psychology was clear and concise, and with some modification for general readership, very suitable for my purpose.

As we have seen, energy manifests in wave form or rhythmic, numerical structures. Colour, like sound, has its particular wave-length, frequency or vibration, which can be expressed numeric-ally. The framework of the horoscope is comprised of universally recognized divisions (the 360 degrees of the ecliptic—the long-itudinal divisions which you can see in any school atlas, and thus represents the conscious attempt of mankind to seek for an under-standing and orientation with life and nature through the orderly (numerical) structures that are inherent in his being.

The Energy Patterns of the Horoscope

To the casual observer, the well-known circle of the horoscope, with its twelve houses and planetary symbols means little or nothing. To the experienced, it becomes a vibrant pattern of energy complexes. In such a graphic framework or blue-print, stress and anxiety may be seen as the more discordant rhythms within the energy patterns. Stress brings about agitation and emotion, which is just another way of describing a process of movement—the result of disharmoniously utilized energy. As we have seen, there are long-established and well-tried methods for redistributing, re-directing and harmonizing the energy complexes, though many people today feel that the only way to cope with life's divine energy is to damp it down with drugs.

Self-realization

And yet, instinctively, the majority of us know there are other ways of reaching the quiet havens of the mind, and that our quest for this ideal lies along the path of knowledge and understanding. We search the world's literature for a glimmer of light, and perhaps draw comfort from some aspect of religion or philosophy. The fact that the process of seeking and striving for understanding is a therapy in itself has been borne in on me, over the years, through my astrology classes at Further Education Centres. True, the client who pays for an analysis avoids the hard work of interpretation, though the effectiveness of the analysis must, inevitably, depend upon the wisdom and insight of the astrologer; but for a student doing a ten- or fifteen-week course, growth in self-understanding proceeds almost imperceptibly alongside the process of learning the astrological techniques.

At the start of a new class there is a natural trepidation. Students ask themselves what they will discover when they look into their own charts—which, of course, is the same as asking what will one find when one is able to look into oneself. A few sit at their desks with unsmiling faces, and usually disappear after the first class or two. These are the ones who maybe take themselves too seriously, but the great majority of us have the ability to laugh at ourselves.

The result of actually looking at a blue-print of our true selves is that we begin to experience ourselves more fully. Life becomes no less challenging, but it does become richer as the horizons of the mind widen out. Moreover, when it is realized that human posturing is rather futile and incongruous in the light of truth, good humour and a philosophical outlook develop of their own accord— a bonus for self-acceptance. Towards the end of each course, students usually exhibit a real enthusiasm over gaining a new-found ability and deeper understanding. I often perceive a fresh sparkle in their eyes that encourages me a great deal. It is as though, through astrology, we are enabled to discern something of the eternal truth about Self. The process of discovery is indeed an exhilarating one. Jung puts it like this: 'Personality is the supreme realization . . . It is an act of high courage flung in the face of life . . .'

The restless, nervous energy of stress and tension becomes transformed into dynamic determination when life's purpose is perceived, and it is the function of all great religions to reveal that purpose. When mankind is deprived of the Church's teaching of the fundamentals of its unique symbology, man seeks desperately elsewhere. In our modern, technocratic age, visions of angels are replaced by 'sightings' of flying-saucers of UFOs. Yet, when we do go to church, be it Christian or Muslim, twelfth-century flint or twentieth-century brick and cement, we still kneel and pray towards the dawn-point of the sun, acknowledging our God, the Creator and Giver of Light. In this act, as in so many other aspects of religion, the unconscious symbolism of universal faith and of astrology run very close together, like an infinite warp of silver thread upon which the golden weft of self-realization may be woven.

BIBLIOGRAPHY

Anderson, M., *The Secret Power of Numbers,* The Aquarian Press, 1972.

Barker, Culver M., *Healing in Depth,* Hodder & Stoughton, 1972.

Benson, H., *The Relaxation Response,* Fountain Books, 1977.

Bono, Edward de, *Lateral Thinking,* Penguin Books/Ward Lock, 1970.

Carter, C. E. O., *An Encyclopaedia of Astrological Psychology,* Theosophical Publishing House London, 1963.

Chapman, J. B., *Biochemistry,* New Era Laboratories Ltd., 1963.

Churchill, Sir W., *Painting as a Pastime,* Odhams Books, 1948.

Ebertin, R., *The Combination of Stellar Influences,* Ebertin-Verlag, 1960.

Franz, M-L von, *Number and Time,* Rider & Co., 1974.

Gauquelin, M., *Cosmic Influences on Human Behaviour,* Garnstone Press, 1973.

Guntrip, H., *Psychology for Ministers and Social Workers,* Allen & Unwin, 1971.

Hill, R., *Bran,* Thorsons Publishers Ltd., 1976.

Jung, C. G., *Analytical Psychology,* Routledge & Kegan Paul, 1968.

—— *The Secret of the Golden Flower,* Routledge & Kegan Paul, 1962.

—— *Man and His Symbols,* Aldus Books Ltd., 1964.

Lawrence, Br., *The Practice of the Presence of God,* S. Bagster & Sons Ltd., London.

Luscher, M., *The Luscher Colour Test,* Jonathan Cape Ltd., 1969.

Mayo, J., *Teach Yourself Astrology,* The English Universities Press Ltd., 1967 (new edition 1980).

—— *The Planets and Human Behaviour,* L. N. Fowler & Co. Ltd., 1972.

Pelt, S. J. van, *Hypnotism,* Foyles Handbooks, 1960.

Reifler, S., *I Ching,* Bantam Books, 1974.

Ross, A. C. G., *Homoeopathy,* Thorsons Publishers Ltd., 1977.

Rudhyar, D., *An Astrological Study of Psychological Complexes and Emotional Problems,* Servire, 1969.

—— *The Astrology of Personality,* Servire, 1963.

—— *The Practice of Astrology,* Servire, 1968.

Sawtell, V., *Astrology and Biochemistry,* Health Science Press, 1975.

Shastri, H. P., *Yoga,* Foyles Handbooks, 1958.

Tangerman, E. J., *Whittling and Woodcarving,* Dover Publications Inc., 1962.

Weekes, C., *Self-Help for Your Nerves,* Angus and Robertson, 1979.

INDEX